Discovering Your Spiritual Path Workbook

Self-Assessments, Exercises & Educational Handouts

Ester A. Leutenberg
John J. Liptak, EdD

Illustrated by
Amy L. Brodsky, LISW-S

D1607184

WholePerson
Mental Health & Wellness
publisher of therapy, counseling, and self-help resources

Whole Person Associates
101 West 2nd Street, Suite 203
Duluth, MN 55802

800-247-6789

Books@WholePerson.com
WholePerson.com

Discovering Your Spiritual Path Workbook
Self-Assessments, Exercises & Educational Handouts

Printed in the United States of America

Editorial Director: Carlene Sippola
Art Director: Joy Morgan Dey

Library of Congress Control Number: 2009941904
ISBN: 978-1-57025-237-2

Dedication

Discovering Your Spiritual Path Workbook is lovingly dedicated to Kathy Atarah Khalsa, who in 1987 lighted the way.

Thanks to the following people who completed our spirituality survey and/or suggested favorite spirituality books for our reference pages in the last chapter:

Manohar Ahuja	Fritz Clarke	Siri-Dya Khalsa	Jim Phillips
Don Anderson	Risa Dorf-Brooks	Allen Klein	Pauline Raymond
Brenda Gottlieb Atkin	Dolores Dowling	Arielle Korb	Joanne Reba
Jeffrey Atkin	Arlyne Druckman	Mason Korb	Eileen Regen
Rondi Atkin	Eric Dunn	Shayna Korb	Scott Regen
Gene Bammel	Lisa Brauer Eisenstat	Judy Krausser	Lucy Ritzic
Stephen Barnusski	Osmond Ekwueme	Corinne Kulick	Carol Rosner
Halle Barnett	Diane Emison	William Kurschinski	Peggy Gawiser Shecket
Jeff Barton	Greg E. Fortier	Tamar Levy	Deborah Schein
Ian Beaton	Lois Frank	Beatrice Lewis	Jeffrey Schein
George Best	Penelope Frese	Douglas Link	Steve Segar
David Birvirt	Harriet Gallen	Anne Lowe	Donald Shields
Joan Birvirt	Chuck George	Christa Lubatkin	Bailey Smith
Joe Bolze	Andy Getz	Mike Lubatkin	Mary Ann Staky
Sandie Bolze	Aurelie Jones Goodwin	Prahaladan Mandelkorn	Julie Stoneberg
Sheli Braun	Bernice Grant	Jack Martin	Cindy Thomas
Joan Brauer	Sheryl Hirsh	Nannie Maxwell	Don Tuski
Jim Briney	Denny Hirsh	Betty Welch McGaughey	Erv Walhof
Sandra Briney	David Hirschhorn	Richard McQuate	Robert Wallin
Amy Brodsky	Ron Hunt	Leona Mitchell	Gerard I.Willger
Carol A. Butler	David Janzen	Kerry Moles	Gayl Woityra
Delores Carl	Robert Jensen	Bruce K. Munro	Joel Wolinsky
Paul Chorney	Leah Kamionkowski	Belleruth Naparstek	Lynne Yulish
Shirley R. Chorney	Kathy Khalsa	Sandra Negley	Fran Zamore
		Abraham Nelson	

Special thanks for the time and expertise of the following professionals whose input in *Discovering Your Spiritual Path Workbook* has been so valuable!

Rev. James Briney, B.A., M. Div.	Corinne Kulick, OTR	Deborah Schein, M.Ed.
Kathy A. Khalsa, MAJS, OTR/L	Kathy Liptak, Ed.D.	Rabbi Jeffrey Schein, Ed.D
Shayna Korb, BS	Eileen Regen, M.Ed., CJE	Rev. Donald Shields, BRE, MTS
	Lucy Ritzic, OTR/L	

With gratitude and ongoing THANK YOUs to:

Amy L. Brodsky, LISW-S

whose creative, thought-provoking illustrations continue to give our workbooks added meaning.

Jay Leutenberg

whose years in the printing business brings the editing and proofreading of our books to a higher level.

Eileen Regen,

an editor, proofreader and consultant extraordinaire.

Carlene Sippola, Publisher, Whole Person Associates

who provides a broad range of products based on a whole person approach that considers mental, emotional, social, spiritual and lifestyle issues. We are so appreciative of her faith in us.

V.I.P. ~ Very Important for the Professional

Our goal

Our goal for *Discovering Your Spiritual Path Workbook's* assessments, activities, journaling pages, quotations and educational handouts is to open participants to the possibilities of spirituality and its benefits. We believe people on a spiritual path lead more healing, enriching, enlightening, peace-filled lives. We interviewed over one hundred people of many different faiths and economic backgrounds. We spoke to people of varied ages, genders, sexual orientations, cultures, nationalities and religions. We were privileged to discuss the topic presented with believers and non-believers and clergy of most every faith before we even began the process of writing this book.

Defining and Addressing Individual Spirituality

Each person we interviewed had different opinions and beliefs about spirituality. Some had none. Our challenging task was opening a topic so complex and immense, and not appearing over simplistic, condescending, incomplete or confusing. Since spirituality can be a sensitive subject, we avoided over-using the word spirituality and we focused on the topics we felt were the components of spirituality, to gather the greatest variety of honest responses and ideas, as well as to encourage a wide range of thought processes.

We asked these questions: Are you . . .

> *1.) spiritual, but not religious?*
> *2.) religious, but not spiritual?*
> *3.) religious and spiritual?*
> *4.) neither religious nor spiritual?*

> *In what way is your spirituality connected with your religion?*
> *How would you define spirituality?*
> *What/where do you feel your spirituality or a genuine warm feeling?*
> *Which situations feel non-spiritual or irritating?*

Shayna Korb, aspacewithin.com, used thematic analysis to create the following categories that represent definitions of spirituality from the one-hundred plus participants who completed our survey:

Healing/Growth — a force toward greater individual or world health

Understanding/Meaning/Answers — the drive towards greater knowing

Connection — a related or connected feeling

Feeling — a particular sense-state, (e.g. a state of flow perceived in quiet moments or moments of meditation)

Force God/Higher Power — some kind of relationship to a higher power

Inner/Within — an internal construction, a knowing inside

Energy/Metaphysics — awareness of an underlying energy or reality undefined by contemporary science

Negative Case — people who do not see themselves as spiritual, define spirituality in a negative way or have no understanding or definition of spirituality at all.

(Continued on the next page)

V.I.P. ~ Very Important for the Professional (page 2)

Defining and Addressing Individual Spirituality (Continued)

Another one of our goals was to find the PERFECT definition of spirituality. Spirituality is a difficult concept to define because it can mean many different things to different people. Defining spirituality is individual and personal. We hope that our readers' felt-sense of spirituality can connect to one or more of the multiple frameworks presented in this text. We believe the chapters in this book reflect components of spirituality that can be useful to everyone, regardless of how they define spirituality.

For the purposes of this book, we define religion as a set of beliefs and practices based on a specific religious doctrine. We attempt to differentiate spirituality from religion. In *Discovering Your Spiritual Path Workbook* we are focusing primarily with spirituality, not religion (although religion can be a part of spirituality). We have purposefully avoided much discussion of religion, allowing the facilitator to use personal judgment to the extent that religion plays a part in this process for each individual.

We have included a handout, *Definitions Of Spirituality*, in the participant's section in this chapter. It consists of several of the definitions from our surveys that seem to represent most of the responses in some way. You may choose to read the definitions aloud to the participants, with the hope that one of the quotations might set off a spark, a thought or an idea for those who are unsure of how to define spirituality. The quotations may help those who do feel some level of spirituality verbalize their ideas. Either way, participants may find something with which to identify. After the definitions page are the handouts *When/Where Do You Feel Your Spirituality or a Genuine Warm Feeling?* and *Which of These Feel Non-Spiritual or Irritating?* These can be used as pre- and post-discussion tools or warm-ups before you begin facilitating the book, afterwards, or both.

The Nature of Spirituality

Wellness includes six important dimensions: occupational, social, emotional, intellectual, physical and spiritual. The spiritual dimension, according to the National Wellness Institute*, recognizes the search for meaning and purpose in human existence. This search includes the development of a deep appreciation for the depth and expanse of life and natural forces that exist in the universe.

It will help to keep several tenets in mind as your clients explore spiritual themes in their lives:

- This spiritual search will be characterized by a peaceful harmony between their internal personal feelings and the external realities that exist in their lives.

- While conducting this search, they may experience feelings of doubt, despair, fear and disappointment as well as feelings of joy, happiness, contentment and discovery. These important experiences and components to their search will be displayed in the value system they adapt to bring meaning to their existence.

- They will know they are becoming spiritual or more spiritual when their actions become more consistent with their beliefs and values, resulting in a "world view."

*Hettler, B. (2004). *Six dimensional model of wellness.* Stevens Point, WI: National Wellness Institute. www.nationalwellness.org.

(Continued on the next page)

The Nature of Spirituality *(Continued)*

In the book, *Spirituality for Dummies**, Sharon Janis suggests some of the ways that spirituality can manifest itself:

- Experiencing a higher universal love
- Surfing the waves of life with a light-hearted view that nurtures a positive sense of humor
- Achieving the ability to see the spiritual in one's ordinary life
- Developing a mature approach to life that includes peacefulness and spirituality
- Experiencing the divine through faith, optimism and an unfettered heart
- Trusting one's own inner guidance

Preparing to Use the Workbook

Discovering Your Spiritual Path Workbook contains five separate sections to help participants learn more about themselves and their spiritual natures. They will learn about the importance of spirituality, their ability to integrate spirituality into their everyday lives, and tools and techniques to enhance their spiritual awareness.

Sections of this book are:

1) Forgiveness and Acceptance Scale helps individuals explore their ability to forgive themselves and forgive other people.

2) Connecting with Others Scale helps individuals explore the strength of their characteristics related to connecting with other people.

3) Spiritual Living Scale helps individuals identify how effective they are at integrating spiritual themes into their daily lives.

4) Personal Centering Scale helps individuals explore their use of the various spiritual disciplines for finding peace and centering themselves, even when facing life's challenges.

5) Spiritual Awareness Scale helps individuals explore how aware they are of their spiritual nature.

6) The Last Chapter helps individuals process what they have learned from *Discovering Your Spiritual Path Workbook*.

The five sections of this book are intended to serve as avenues for individual self-reflection, as well as for group experiences revolving around identified topics of importance. Each assessment includes directions for easy administration, scoring and interpretation, and provides exploratory activities, reflective journaling activities, related quotations and educational handouts. All materials have been designed to help participants discover their spirituality in a variety of ways.

**Janis, S. (2008) *Spirituality for Dummies*. Wiley, John & Sons, Inc.

The Assessments, Journaling Activities, Quotations and Educational Handouts

The art of self-reflection goes back many centuries and is rooted in many of the world's greatest spiritual and philosophical traditions. Socrates, the ancient Greek philosopher, was known to walk the streets engaging the people he met in philosophical reflection and dialogue. He felt that this type of activity was so important in life that he went so far as to proclaim, "The unexamined life is not worth living!" The unexamined life is one in which the same routine is continually repeated without ever thinking about its meaning to one's life and how this life really could be lived. However, a structured reflection and examination of beliefs, assumptions, characteristics, and patterns can provide a better understanding, which can lead to a more satisfying life. A greater level of self-understanding about important life skills is often necessary to make positive, self-directed changes in the over-used or repetitious patterns. The assessments and exercises in this book can help promote this self-understanding. Through involvement in the in-depth activities, the participant claims ownership in the development of positive patterns.

Journaling is an extremely powerful tool for enhancing self-discovery, learning, transcending traditional problems, breaking ineffective life habits, and helping to heal from psychological traumas of the past. From a physical point of view, writing reduces stress and lowers muscle tension, blood pressure and heart rate levels. Psychologically, writing reduces sadness, depression and general anxiety, and leads it to a greater level of life satisfaction and optimism. Behaviorally, writing leads to enhanced social skills, emotional intelligence and creativity. It also leads to improved writing skills which, in turn, leads to more self-confidence in the workplace. By combining reflective assessment and journaling, participants will be exposed to a powerful method of combining verbalizing and writing to reflect on and solve problems. Participants will become more aware of their spiritual strengths. They will explore ways to develop strategies to acquire an additional dimension in their lives with which to face life's challenges and enhance their daily lives.

Preparation for using the assessments and activities in this book is important. In order for you to be effective in administering the assessments in this book, it is suggested that you, the facilitator, complete them yourself. This will familiarize you with the format of the assessments, the scoring directions, the interpretation guides and the journaling activities. Although the assessments are designed to be self-administered, scored and interpreted. This familiarity will help prepare facilitators to answer participants' questions about the assessments.

The Assessments, Journaling Activities, Quotations and Educational Handouts in *Discovering Your Spiritual Path Workbook* are reproducible and ready to be photocopied for participants' use.

The Assessments, Journaling Activities, Quotations and Educational Handouts *(page 2)*

Assessments contained in this book focus on self-reported data and can be used as materials for individual self-inventory, partner study, spirituality study groups, classes and therapeutic supplements by psychologists, counselors, therapists, clergy, religious and spiritual leaders and teachers, activity directors and career consultants.

Accuracy and usefulness of the information provided is dependent on the truthful information that each participant provides through self-examination. By being honest, participants help themselves discover their life patterns and uncover information that might be keeping them from expanding the dimension of their spiritual path on the wellness continuum.

An assessment instrument can provide participants with valuable information about themselves; however, it cannot measure or identify everything about them. The purposes of the assessments is not to pigeon-hole certain characteristics, but rather to allow participants to explore all of their characteristics. *Discovering Your Spiritual Path Workbook* contains self-assessments, not tests. Tests measure knowledge or whether something is right or wrong. For the assessments in this book, there are no right or wrong answers. These assessments ask for personal opinions or attitudes about a topic of importance in the participant's spiritual nature.

When administering assessments in this workbook, remember that the items are generically written so that they will be applicable to a wide variety of people but will not account for every possible variable for every person.

Advise the participants taking the assessments that they should not spend too much time trying to analyze the content of the questions; their initial response will most likely be true. Regardless of individual scores, encourage participants to talk about their findings and their feelings pertaining to what they have discovered about themselves. Talking about the components of spirituality can enhance the lives of participants. These exercises can be used by group facilitators working with any population who may want to explore their spirituality, or with those whom you feel would be open and able to benefit from exploring a spiritual path.

The Assessments, Journaling Activities, Quotations and Educational Handouts (page 3)

Layout of the Book

- **Assessment Instrument** — Self-assessment inventories with scoring directions and interpretation materials. Group facilitators can choose one or more of the activities relevant to their participants.

- **Activity Handouts** — Practical questions and activities to prompt self-reflection and promote self-understanding. These questions and activities foster introspection and promote pro-social behaviors.

- **Reflective Questions for Journaling** — Self-exploration activities and journaling exercises specific to each assessment to enhance self-discovery, learning and healing.

- **Educational Handout** — Handouts designed to supplement instruction can be used individually or in groups. They can be distributed, converted into masters for overheads or transparencies, or written on a board and discussed.

- **Quotations** — Quotations are included throughout the chapters to motivate and inspire, as well as promote self-reflection and provide insight into the thoughts of various spiritual leaders.

Who Should Use This Program?

This book has been designed as a practical tool for helping professional therapists, counselors, career counselors and coaches, psychologists, teachers, spiritual and religious leaders, and group leaders help their clients. Depending on the role of the professional using *Discovering Your Spiritual Path Workbook* and the specific group's needs, these sections can be used individually, combined, or implemented as part of an integrated curriculum for a more comprehensive approach.

Why Use Self-Assessments?

Self-assessments are important in teaching various life skills. Participants will . . .

- Become aware of the primary motivators that guide their behavior.

- Explore and learn to indentify challenging situations.

- Explore the effects of messages received in childhood.

- Gain insight that will guide greater understanding of one's spirituality.

- Focus thinking on behavioral goals for expanding one's spirituality.

- Uncover spiritual resources that can help one to cope with problems and difficulties.

- Explore personal characteristics without judgment.

- Develop full awareness of personal strengths and spiritual understanding.

Because the assessments are presented in a straightforward and easy-to-use format, individuals can self-administer, score and understand each assessment independently.

Introduction for the Participant

The intent of *Discovering Your Spiritual Path Workbook* is to either start you on your spirituality path or assist you in enriching your present spiritual path. Your spiritual path is an ever-moving and changing aspect of life.

Spirituality is hard to define. We have discovered that it is often what each person believes it to be — and that one's perception of spirituality can change over and over again. In interviews with over one hundred people, we found each person's definition was different from the others — and yet, each person's definition is correct as a personal understanding. Many people connect their religion with spirituality and some think religion and spirituality are different. We hope when you are finished with this book, you are able to create your own definition of spirituality or to expand on the definition you already have.

Spirituality is a critical component of the overall concept of wellness. Spiritual wellness has been described as a process of getting in touch with your inner self by exploring the spiritual themes in your life and thereby discovering your personal spiritual ideas and understandings. As you begin to further develop these dimensions of your life, you will have many questions, and we hope you will find many answers. You may also learn to embrace mystery, and value things that you do not completely understand. Spiritual wellness is about becoming more peaceful and compassionate, and connecting deeply with yourself and others, as well as developing spiritual wisdom and spiritual virtues.

Discovering Your Spiritual Path Workbook is designed to help you learn more about yourself, to guide your considerations of the notions of spirituality in your life, and explore ways you can use to enhance the spiritual dimension of your life. We truly hope that you will be able to find some of the answers you seek and discover hidden knowledge you may not even know you possess. We hope that you use this workbook to find meaning, purpose, optimism, peace and contentment in your life.

Enjoy the spiritual journey!

Let's Begin

The next three pages include activities to help you get started in exploring your spiritual path. It might be fun for you to complete these three exercises now and then again after you have completed the book. It will be interesting to see if and how your responses change. *Review the Definitions of Spirituality* page and then complete the two worksheets that follow.

For the Participants ~ Definitions of Spirituality

Random selections from our collection of over 100 surveys and interviews

Spirituality is an avenue of healing, inspiration and practical growth in living one's life. It can include drawing on and from the depths of one's religious faith and revelations since youth. But spirituality need not be religious at all. One can be very spiritual by nature and never talk about God, religion or scripture. Sacredness, love and joy are the common side effects of refined awareness, which is spirituality. ~ P. Mandelkorn

Spirituality is the primal human longing for meaning and a way to organize both our inner and outer world of feeling, stories, memories and experiences. ~ D. Shields

Spirituality is a connected feeling: Connected deeply to myself and connected to something larger than myself. ~ K. Khalsa

Spirituality for me is a feeling of awe, wonderment and connectedness to the universe – to those I love, dead and alive. ~ E. Leutenberg

Spirituality, for me, is the sense of what is beyond me, what is "greater" than me, what is as yet unknown, a mystery or unexplainable. It is the search for making meaning out of the things that are known – the realities of my life – all in the context of the bigger picture. It is both understanding that very little is in my control and taking responsibility for what I can control and affect. It is living as authentically as I can in accordance with my values. So, it is both an interior life, and the outward expression of that life. ~ J. Stoneberg

My sense of my own spirituality includes a sense of the interdependent web of life, of which I am a small part. This includes a source of universal energy that holds wisdom and power beyond what I or any one person can imagine. It is always there and available to me, if I open my heart and mind, and silence my thoughts to listen. ~ A. Goodwin

For me, spirituality is the indefinable connection that I might know, or feel, or intuit with that Oneness that is everything. Certain quantum physics theories help us understand mentally that we are all energy and all energy is connected. Certainly when you feel that connectedness, you will live and act with respect, reverence and gratitude. Hence, spirituality is involved with behaviors, attitudes and values. ~ G. Woityra

Spirituality is the feeling of the presence and essence of God during every day of my life. ~ A. Druckman

Spirituality is my connection with the "beyond" that we are all a part of. It is a sense of who I am in relationship to others, living, dead and still unborn. It is a sense of purpose in this life. It is a conviction that there are no coincidences and we each have a soul's purpose; things happen for a reason – to elevate us and give us the opportunity to reach our highest purpose and potential. ~ F. Zamore

Spirituality is the depth dimension of your experience. It is an awakening, an awareness, a heightened experience of being more fully alive. ~ G. Bammel

Circle any of the above to which you can relate.
If you have a personal definition of spirituality, please write it here:

_____

_____

_____

_____

For the Participants

When/where do you feel your spirituality or a genuine warm feeling?

Check those that apply to you below	Write your own examples in these 2 columns	
In nature:	**In nature:**	
__ Animals	_____	_____
__ Unique moments	_____	_____
__ Weather	_____	_____
__ Bodies of water	_____	_____
__ A tree or flower in blossom	_____	_____
With my religion:	**With my religion:**	
__ House of worship	_____	_____
__ Prayer	_____	_____
__ Traditions and rituals	_____	_____
__ Sacred texts	_____	_____
__ Holidays	_____	_____
Within my body's experiences:	**Within my body's experiences:**	
__ Sports	_____	_____
__ Exercises	_____	_____
__ Yoga/Martial arts	_____	_____
__ Relaxation techniques	_____	_____
__ Solitude	_____	_____
In self-expression:	**In self-expression:**	
__ Creating	_____	_____
__ Music	_____	_____
__ Writing	_____	_____
__ Singing	_____	_____
__ Art	_____	_____
In relationships:	**In relationships:**	
__ Awareness of affection	_____	_____
__ Communicating heart to heart	_____	_____
__ Taking action to make a difference	_____	_____
__ Being in sync with my partner	_____	_____
__ Enjoying intimate moments	_____	_____
With myself:	**With myself:**	
__ AHA! Moments	_____	_____
__ Illness	_____	_____
__ Slowing down, deep breaths	_____	_____
__ Thankfulness	_____	_____
__ Belief in my own value	_____	_____
Other:	**Other:**	
_____	_____	_____
_____	_____	_____
_____	_____	_____
_____	_____	_____

For the Participants

Situations which feel non-spiritual or irritating?

Check off below	Write your own examples in these 2 columns	
__ Arguments	_____	_____
__ Athletic events	_____	_____
__ Bad speaker	_____	_____
__ Bureaucracy	_____	_____
__ Bigotry	_____	_____
__ Busy places	_____	_____
__ Chaos	_____	_____
__ Dishonesty	_____	_____
__ Disloyalty	_____	_____
__ Frustration	_____	_____
__ Gossip	_____	_____
__ Hate	_____	_____
__ Human's inhumanity to human	_____	_____
__ Ignorance	_____	_____
__ Jealousy	_____	_____
__ Local news	_____	_____
__ Media	_____	_____
__ Noise	_____	_____
__ Not enough time	_____	_____
__ Paperwork	_____	_____
__ Pettiness	_____	_____
__ Physical sickness	_____	_____
__ Political games	_____	_____
__ Prejudicial thinking	_____	_____
__ Racism	_____	_____
__ Rock music	_____	_____
__ Selfishness	_____	_____
__ Shopping	_____	_____
__ Soap operas	_____	_____
__ Times of stress	_____	_____
__ Violence	_____	_____
__ Waiting in lines	_____	_____
__ War	_____	_____
__ Worry	_____	_____
__ Yelling	_____	_____

How can you avoid these situations, or be less irritated by them?

_____

_____

_____

_____

TABLE OF CONTENTS

TABLE OF CONTENTS *(continued)*

TABLE OF CONTENTS (continued)

TABLE OF CONTENTS *(continued)*

SECTION I:
Forgiveness & Acceptance Scale

NAME _____   DATE _____

You have the opportunity to forgive both yourself and other people. Forgiveness is a conscious decision to let go of resentments, thoughts of anger, and revenge related to an offense committed against you, or for offenses you committed to yourself or others. Forgiveness is not the same as forgetting what has happened. It just means that by embracing forgiveness, you will reduce the negative feelings you have about what happened and move to a happier and freer life in the present. The Forgiveness & Acceptance Scale can help you explore your thoughts, feelings and actions related to forgiveness — both forgiving yourself and forgiving others.

Forgiveness is an act of the will, a choice and a decision.

> **This chapter is unique in that it contains two separate assessments, one that helps you identify how effective you are in forgiving yourself and one that helps you identify how effective you are in forgiving others.**

Forgiveness & Acceptance

Self-Forgiveness Scale Directions

Think about a past instance or situation for which you are having trouble forgiving yourself. Describe that instance or situation:

_____

_____

For the Self-Forgiveness Scale that follows, answer the questions on the instance or situation you provided above.

This scale contains 40 statements related to the process of forgiving and accepting yourself. Read each of the statements and decide whether or not the statement describes you. If the statement is true, circle the number next to that item under the TRUE column.
If the statement is false, circle the number next to that item under the FALSE column.

In the following example, the circled number under FALSE indicates the statement is not true of the person completing the inventory.

	TRUE	FALSE
(A) I accept myself as I am with all my problems and limitations.	2	(1)

This is not a test and there are no right or wrong answers. Do not spend too much time thinking about your answers. Your initial response will likely be the most true for you. Be sure to respond to every statement.

(Turn to the next page and begin)

Self-Forgiveness Scale

Focus on the past instance or situation that you stated in the box on the previous page and indicate whether or not the statement is true or false for you in this instance or situation.

	TRUE	FALSE
(A) I accept myself as I am with all my problems and limitations	2	1
(A) I cannot let go of blaming myself for my mistakes	1	2
(A) I can finally let go of my guilt	2	1
(A) I often engage in negative self name-calling	1	2
(A) I can, and do, trust in my own goodness, no matter what	2	1
(A) I have terrible remorse	1	2
(A) I seem to have lost the love for myself	1	2
(A) I am so sad, I can't let it go	1	2

(A) Total _____

	TRUE	FALSE
(B) I feel angry a lot when I think about this incident	1	2
(B) I know that I did the best that I could at that time	2	1
(B) I feel that the other person doesn't deserve my forgiveness	1	2
(B) I keep replaying the incident in my mind	1	2
(B) I rarely act out in self-destructive ways	2	1
(B) I blame myself for my part in this incident	1	2
(B) I want to make myself pay for what happened	1	2
(B) I hate myself for what happened	1	2

(B) Total _____

	TRUE	FALSE
(C) I now understand what happened	2	1
(C) I understand why I did what I did	2	1
(C) It is hard for me to find anything good about myself	1	2
(C) I am beginning to move from the feelings of victim and/or guilt to empowerment	2	1
(C) I cannot separate the past from the present	1	2
(C) I am aware that this incident might not have been my fault	2	1
(C) I have become aware of how my pain from the past affected my reaction to this incident	2	1
(C) I understand and accept that life is not always fair	2	1

(C) Total _____

(Continued on the next page)

(Self-Forgiveness Scale *continued*)

	TRUE	FALSE
(D) I have accepted and forgiven myself for what happened	2	1
(D) I am able to see the situation differently	2	1
(D) I cannot find meaning in what happened	1	2
(D) I have released all my resentment	2	1
(D) I have not found peace since the incident	1	2
(D) I got what I deserved	2	1
(D) I refuse to let the past interfere with my life	2	1
(D) I have accepted what happened	2	1

(D) Total _____

	TRUE	FALSE
(E) I try not to think about what happened	1	2
(E) I just deny that anything happened	1	2
(E) I am able to put this incident out of my mind	2	1
(E) I have not been able to forget this incident	1	2
(E) I live as if this incident never existed	1	2
(E) I am too ashamed to think about this incident	1	2
(E) I try not to feel guilty when I think about this incident	2	1
(E) I try not to think about this incident because it is so painful	1	2

(E) Total _____

(Go to the Scoring Directions on the next page)

Self-Forgiveness Scale Scoring Directions

Self-forgiveness is a decision that you can make to let go of resentments about something you did, or feel you did, in the past.

Self-forgiveness is not a one-step event, but a process to work through — a journey on which you must embark. It will not be easy, but you must know where you currently are. The Forgiveness & Acceptance Scale is designed to assess where you are in the self-forgiveness process. To get your (A) Forgiving Yourself score, total the numbers you circled for statements marked (A) on the scale. You will get a score from 8 to 16. Put that number on the line next to the (A) Total line on the scale you just completed. Do the same for the next four scales: (B), (C), (D) and (E). Then transfer those numbers below.

(A) Forgiving Yourself Total   = _____

(B) Anger Total   = _____

(C) Understanding/Insight Total   = _____

(D) Acceptance/Compassion Total   = _____

(E) Denial/Avoidance Total   = _____

Profile Interpretation

TOTAL SCALES SCORES	RESULT	INDICATIONS
Scores from 14 to 16	High	You have been able to overcome the sadness associated with the incident or situation and you are well on the way to forgiving yourself and finding inner peace.
Scores from 11 to 13	Moderate	You have been able to overcome some of the sadness associated with the incident or situation but you can still work on forgiving yourself and finding inner peace.
Scores from 8 to 10	Low	You are having difficulty overcoming the sadness associated with the incident or situation and you need assistance to work on forgiving yourself and finding inner peace, and you will benefit by completing the activities that follow.

Self-Forgiveness Scale Descriptions

SCALE A – Forgiving Yourself

People scoring low on this scale indicate they are unable to forgive themselves. They forget that everyone makes mistakes at times and they need to forgive themselves. They need to learn to be courageous, loving to themselves and ready to forgive themselves as well as other people.

SCALE B – Anger

People scoring low on this scale indicate they continue to feel angry about what happened. They are angry at themselves. They keep rethinking the incident which makes them even angrier. They want to do something that would make them feel okay. They feel hurt and angry and may be prone to strike out at themselves both mentally and physically.

SCALE C – Understanding/Insight

People scoring low on this scale indicate they have trouble separating the past from the present and continue to harbor negative feelings about what happened. They still may think they were responsible for what happened and continue to let the pain of the past interfere with their present lives. They may even think that life isn't fair and they will never let go of what happened.

SCALE D – Acceptance/Compassion

People scoring low on this scale seem to be unable to feel compassion for themselves and unable to accept what happened. They cannot find meaning in what happened, and are unable to let go of the need to re-enact what happened. They feel no self-compassion and are unable to see the bigger picture of their value.

SCALE E – Denial/Avoidance

People scoring low on this scale indicate they are still in a state of denial about something that happened in the past. They are having trouble feeling the full impact of what happened and how the incident has influenced their lives. They may be feeling guilty and just want to try to forget that it happened at all. They attempt to overcome these feelings by denying that something happened or by running away from, or ignoring, their feelings.

Self-Forgiveness

Self-forgiveness (forgiving ourselves for what we did, or perceive our action or reaction), cleanses us and allows us to overcome our guilt and shame.

The following method may help you to forgive yourself.

A Question to Consider:

1) What makes it so difficult to forgive yourself?

_____

_____

_____

_____

Start the Forgiveness Process: Try to Forgive Yourself

2) What possible benefits or gains are you receiving from not forgiving yourself?

_____

_____

_____

_____

3) Start the forgiveness process by trying to forgive yourself.
For what do you want to forgive yourself?

_____

_____

_____

Now, forgive yourself out loud for these things!

4) Think of a time that you forgave someone. How can you work on trying to do the same for yourself?

_____

_____

_____

_____

Remember that self-forgiveness is a powerful survival tool. Use it to empower yourself!

Forgiveness & Acceptance

Forgiving Others Scale Directions

Think about a past instance or situation for which you are having trouble forgiving a person for something he or she did to you.

Who is the person you want to forgive, but have not been able to?

_____

Describe a typical instance or situation with that person:

_____

_____

Answer the following questions in the FORGIVING OTHERS SCALE based on the information you provided above.

This scale contains 32 statements related to forgiving others for things they have done in the past. Read each of the statements and decide whether or not the statement describes you. If the statement is true, circle the number next to that item under the TRUE column. If the statement is false, circle the number next to that item under the FALSE column.

In the following example, the circled number under FALSE indicates the statement is not true of the person completing the inventory.

	TRUE	FALSE
(B) I often feel angry	1	(2)

This is not a test and there are no right or wrong answers. Do not spend too much time thinking about your answers. Your initial response will likely be the most true for you. Be sure to respond to every statement.

(Turn to the next page and begin)

Forgiving Others Scale

Focus on the past instance or situation that you stated in the box on the previous page and indicate whether or not the statement is true or false for you in this instance or situation.

	TRUE	FALSE
(A) I often feel angry	1	2
(A) I rarely want to get even	2	1
(A) I want to make the person(s) suffer like I did	1	2
(A) I want the offender to learn a lesson	1	2
(A) I keep replaying it in my mind	1	2
(A) I rarely act out in destructive ways	2	1
(A) I also blame myself for what happened	1	2
(A) I hate the person(s) for what happened	1	2

(A) Total _____

	TRUE	FALSE
(B) I now understand what happened	2	1
(B) I understand why the person(s) did that	2	1
(B) I cannot see positive qualities in the person(s)	1	2
(B) I am beginning to move from victim to empowered	2	1
(B) I cannot separate the past from the present	1	2
(B) I have no reason to feel guilty	2	1
(B) I have become aware of how my pain from the past is affecting my current life	2	1
(B) I understand and accept that life is not always fair	2	1

(B) Total _____

(Continued on the next page)

(Self-Forgiveness Scale *continued*)

	TRUE	FALSE
(C) I have accepted what happened	2	1
(C) I refuse to let the past interfere with my life	2	1
(C) I am able to reverse roles and see the situation differently	2	1
(C) I cannot find meaning in what happened	1	2
(C) I have released all my resentment	2	1
(C) I have not found peace since the incident	1	2
(C) I have forgiven the person(s)	2	1
(C) I have accepted what has happened	2	1

(C) Total _____

	TRUE	FALSE
(D) I keep as much distance as possible	1	2
(D) I just deny that anything happened	1	2
(D) I keep waiting for the other person to express remorse	1	2
(D) I have not been able to forgive	1	2
(D) I live as if this incident never happened	1	2
(D) I am too embarrassed to think about this incident	1	2
(D) I do not feel guilty when I think about this incident	2	1
(D) I try not think about it because this incident is so painful	1	2

(D) Total _____

(Go to the Scoring Directions on the next page)

Forgiving Others Scale Scoring Directions

The assessment you just completed is designed to help you understand where you are in the process of forgiving someone else. This is not a one-step event but a process. It will not be easy, but it is important for you to know where you are currently in the forgiveness process.

To get your (A) Anger/Revenge score, total the numbers you circled for statements marked (A), on the scale. You will get a score from 8 to 16. Put that number on the line next to the (A) Total line on the scale you just completed. Do the same for the next 3 scales: (B), (C) and (D). Then transfer those numbers below.

(A) Anger / Revenge Total   = _____

(B) Understanding / Insight Total   = _____

(C) Acceptance / Compassion Total = _____

(D) Denial / Avoidance Total   = _____

Profile Interpretation

TOTAL SCALES SCORES	RESULT	INDICATIONS
Scores from 14 to 36	High	You have been able to overcome the grudges and bitterness associated with the hurtful incident, and you are well on the way to forgiving those who have hurt you and finding your own inner peace.
Scores from 11 to 13	Moderate	You have been able to overcome some of the grudges and bitterness associated with the hurtful incident, and you are on the way to forgiving those who have hurt you and to finding your own inner peace.
Scores from 8 to 10	Low	You have not been able to overcome the grudges and bitterness associated the harmful incident, and you need additional assistance in order to forgive those who have hurt you and to help you find your own inner peace.

Forgiving Others Scale Descriptions

SCALE A – Anger/Revenge

People scoring low on this scale seem to continue to feel angry about hurtful events in the past. They may be angry at themselves or the perpetrator(s), and they may seek revenge on the other party. They keep replaying the incident in their heads which makes them even angrier. They want to get even and feel like that would make them feel better. They feel hurt and angry and may be prone to strike out in destructive ways.

SCALE B – Understanding/Insight

People scoring low on this scale seem to have trouble separating the past from the present and continue to harbor negative feelings about hurtful events in the past. They still may think they too were responsible for what happened and continue to let the pain of the past interfere with their present lives. They may even think that life "just isn't fair" and they can never let go of what happened.

SCALE C – Acceptance/Compassion

People scoring low on this scale seem to be unable to feel compassion for the other party and unable to accept hurtful events in the past. They cannot find meaning or have empathy for the other party, and are unable to let go of the need to re-enact what happened. They feel no compassion and are unable to see the bigger picture of their lives.

SCALE D – Denial/Avoidance

People scoring low on this scale seem to still be in a state of denial about hurtful events in the past. They are having trouble feeling the full impact of what happened and how the incident has influenced their lives. They may also be feeling guilty at themselves and just want to try to forget that it happened at all. They attempt to overcome these feelings by denying that something happened or by running away from their feelings. Avoidance of the offending person(s) may be a way of coping.

Forgiveness Exercises

Being willing to accept what has happened to you and being willing to forgive other people can bring you a sense of well-being and peace. Regardless of your score on the assessment, the following exercises have been designed to help you forgive people in your life.

Most people do not forgive because they are unaware of what forgiveness truly can incite. Forgiveness can be the refusal to try and do to another what has been done to you. It can be your desire to stop the need for revenge for something that has happened to you.

People often feel as if they have been victimized at some time in their lives. Whether the victimization you experienced was from crime, neglect, accident, childhood abuse, poor family relationships, partner abuse, domineering relationship, alcohol abuse, or something totally different, you need to decide whether or not you will forgive yourself and the offending person(s).

Forgiveness is a gift that you can give to yourself and to anyone who has hurt you or yours, without any conditions attached. Most people think that forgiveness takes place when someone asks for forgiveness for doing something hurtful or wrong. It is healthier not to worry about being asked for forgiveness. You can provide forgiveness to people who have wronged you without their even knowing you have forgiven them. Forgiveness is a gift you give to yourself as well as to the other person(s).

Stifling anger and resentment can cause many physical and psychological problems; forgiveness, however, can become part of the healing process. By forgiving others, you agree to accept a wrong committed against you and move on with your life. Complete the following table of people (they can be living or deceased) whom you feel it might be wise for you to forgive.

People It Might be Wise for Me to Forgive

Person to be forgiven	What the person did
Ex. My mother	Ex. She didn't have time for me

Destructive Thoughts, Behaviors and Feelings

Many destructive thoughts, behaviors and feelings are associated with the inability to forgive people. Destructive thoughts, behaviors and feelings include anger, resentment, a desire for revenge, depression, anxiety, betrayal and self-doubt. List some of the destructive thoughts, behaviors and feelings associated with incidents you listed in the previous table.

What was done to me	Destructive thoughts, behaviors and feelings
Ex. My mother didn't have time to listen to me or help me with my homework when I was young.	*Ex. I was sarcastic and withdrawn from her, even after I grew up. I wished that someone else was my mother and I told her so.*

I Forgive You

In the table below, note the people from the first table whom you would like to forgive. Then in the column on the right, write your statement of forgiveness to them.

Person to be forgiven	My forgiveness statement
Ex. My mom	Ex. Even though you didn't have much time with me when I was young, I now realize that you were a single mother with three children and came home exhausted from work. I now know that you did the best you could. You always had a meal on the table for us and we were safe.

Reconciliation

Forgiveness does not mean that you absolutely must reconcile with someone who has treated you poorly. Forgiveness can be a truly internal process for you. When you forgive someone, you can primarily do it for yourself. Forgiveness does not require you to contact that person. It can be internal forgiveness or with the person's knowledge. However, you may find people from your list that you might like to forgive in person or by writing an email or letter.

Write the names of those people in the spaces below.

Person to be forgiven	When, where and how I will forgive the person

Learning to Forgive

Forgiveness is essential to your spiritual path and your feeling of wellness. Learning to forgive is a process. It is a skill that you can learn and you will discover that it can be easier than it seems.

The following is designed to teach you a method for practicing forgiveness.

1) Start with practicing forgiveness for minor infractions against you. These are relatively easy to forgive things, like a person cutting in front of you in the grocery line or someone throwing garbage on your lawn. List some of the minor things that people have done to you that you could forgive.

Ex. My neighbor yelled at me when my trash can blew onto his lawn. I've been angry at him for two years.

_____

_____

_____

_____

_____

_____

2) Spend a day forgiving all of the negative things that happen to you that day. Become aware of how you feel when you forgive someone rather than dwelling on it and carrying a grudge about it. Write about what you forgave and how it felt:

_____

_____

_____

_____

_____

_____

3) Notice the ways in which you judge other people. These judgments often make forgiveness more difficult. On the next page, list the people whom you tend to judge and how you judge them.

Judging People

People I judge	How I judge them
(Ex. My partner)	*(Ex. I have high expectations and expect her to live up to them. I get angry and have a difficult time forgiving her when she does not.)*

Forgiveness Quotations

Choose two quotes below. On the lines that follow each of those quotes, describe what the quotes mean to you and how it relates to YOUR forgiveness process.

The weak can never forgive. Forgiveness is the attribute of the strong.

~ **Mahatma Gandhi**

_____

_____

_____

Hanging onto resentment is letting someone you despise live rent-free in your head.

~ **Ann Landers**

_____

_____

_____

It is easier to forgive an enemy than to forgive a friend.

~ **William Blake**

_____

_____

_____

Anger makes you smaller, while forgiveness forces you to grow beyond what you were.

~ **Cherie Carter-Scott**

_____

_____

_____

The day the child realizes that all adults are imperfect, he becomes an adolescent. The day he forgives them, he becomes an adult. The day he forgives himself, he becomes wise.

~ **Alden Nowlan**

_____

_____

_____

Forgiveness Letter

Write a letter to the person or people that you would like to forgive the most. Tell them how you feel about what happened, and how you have come to accept and forgive. You do not have to give, mail or email this letter unless you want to.

_____

_____

_____

_____

_____

_____

_____

_____

_____

_____

_____

_____

_____

_____

_____

_____

_____

_____

_____

_____

_____

Benefits of Forgiving

- Spiritual feeling of well-being

- Ability to see the wrong-doer in a new light

- Anger management skills improve

- Control of one's life strengthened

- Emotional health enhanced

- Encouragement of healing

- Freedom from painful memories

- Inner peace develops

- Maturity

- Opportunity to move forward

- Physical wellness improves

- Self-love blossoms

- Stress reduction

It's time to forgive when you . . .

- become consumed with revenge.

- continue to dwell on the incident.

- feel anxious in certain situations.

- feel emotional pain over the incident.

- feel like a victim.

- feel very upset when you see that person.

- find yourself avoiding people.

- frequently dream about the incident.

- anger easily.

- keep trying, without results, to forget the incident.

- regret the loss of a valued relationship.

SECTION II:
Connecting with Others Scale

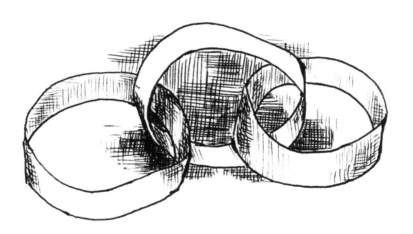

NAME _____   DATE _____

Connecting with Others Scale Directions

Honesty, integrity, humility, compassion and gratitude are the cornerstones of any effective relationship.

The Connecting with Others Scale is designed to measure these characteristics, help you to make better use of the ones you have developed, and help you to be aware of some characteristics you have yet to develop. The assessment contains 40 statements divided into five sections. Read each statement and decide how true the statement is for you. In the following example, the circled 2 indicates that the statement is Somewhat True for the person completing the inventory:

	Mostly True	Somewhat True	Not True
SECTION I: Honesty			
I do not lie by omitting the truth	3	(2)	1

This is not a test and there are no right or wrong answers. Do not spend too much time thinking about your answers. Your initial response will likely be the most true for you. Be sure to respond to every statement.

(Turn to the next page and begin)

Connecting with Others Scale

	Mostly True	Somewhat True	Not True
SECTION I: Honesty			
I do not lie by omitting the truth	3	2	1
I know inside of me what is true	3	2	1
Other people consider me trustworthy	3	2	1
I cannot trust a person who is not honest	3	2	1
I do not give false impressions	3	2	1
I am truthful in a kind and caring way	3	2	1
I am honest about my feelings	3	2	1
I rarely put on a false front for others	3	2	1

TOTAL = _____

	Mostly True	Somewhat True	Not True
SECTION II: Integrity			
I do not regard others as inferior to me	3	2	1
I value human relationships more than money	3	2	1
I show regard for the worth of each person	3	2	1
I stick to what I believe in	3	2	1
I keep my word	3	2	1
I am proud of the way I lead my life	3	2	1
I often take a stand for my moral principles	3	2	1
My actions are consistent with my values	3	2	1

TOTAL = _____

(Continued on the next page)

(Connecting with Others Scale *continued*)

	Mostly True	Somewhat True	Not True

SECTION III: Humility

	Mostly True	Somewhat True	Not True
I believe I am humble	3	2	1
I don't often brag about myself	3	2	1
I don't try to impress other people	3	2	1
I like to be helpful to people, but don't need to be acknowledged	3	2	1
I give credit to and acknowledge others	3	2	1
I do not blame others when things go wrong	3	2	1
I take responsibility for my choices	3	2	1
I am modest about my accomplishments	3	2	1

TOTAL = _____

SECTION IV: Compassion

	Mostly True	Somewhat True	Not True
I usually have empathy for other people	3	2	1
I want to help people less fortunate than I am	3	2	1
I feel what other people are feeling	3	2	1
I feel a commitment to caring for others	3	2	1
I put myself in others' shoes and see their side	3	2	1
I work towards peace and elimination of suffering	3	2	1
I want to work for the good of humanity	3	2	1
I like to help people of all races, religions, cultures, etc.	3	2	1

TOTAL = _____

SECTION V: Gratitude

	Mostly True	Somewhat True	Not True
I give thanks everyday for the blessings in my life	3	2	1
I am grateful when I receive any kind of help or support	3	2	1
I have very much to be grateful for	3	2	1
I often reflect on how fortunate I am	3	2	1
I let people know how grateful I am to and for them	3	2	1
I say Thank You often and sincerely	3	2	1
I focus on my good luck	3	2	1
I do not feel resentment for things I do not have	3	2	1

TOTAL = _____

(Go to the Scoring Directions on the next page)

Connecting with Others Scale
Scoring Directions

People who are well connected to others exhibit certain critical spiritual virtues, and thus they are able to interact with others and form concrete bonds. They believe that all people are interconnected and that by helping others, they are helping themselves. For each of the sections on the previous pages, total the scores you circled for each of the sections. Put that total on the TOTAL at the end of each section.

Then, transfer your totals to the spaces below:

SECTION I   TOTAL   =   _____   (Honesty)

SECTION II   TOTAL   =   _____   (Integrity)

SECTION III TOTAL   =   _____   (Humility)

SECTION IV   TOTAL   =   _____   (Compassion)

SECTION V   TOTAL   =   _____   (Gratitude)

Profile Interpretation

TOTAL SCALES SCORES	RESULT	INDICATIONS
Scores from 8 to 13	Low	You probably possess only a few of the characteristics needed to be able to connect with other people, but you can develop more. Developing these characteristics will help you to connect with other people in a more intimate and spiritual way.
Scores from 14 to 18	Moderate	You probably possess some of the characteristics needed to be able to connect with other people. Work to develop these characteristics to help you connect with other people in a more intimate and spiritual way.
Scores from 19 to 24	High	You seem to possess many of the characteristics needed to be able to connect with other people. Continue to strengthen these characteristics to connect with other people in a more intimate and spiritual way.

The higher your score on each of the scales of this assessment, the more you are able to connect spiritually with other people using that particular virtue. In the areas in which you score in the **Moderate** or **Low** range, make efforts to continue to develop and strengthen these characteristics. No matter if you scored **Low**, **Moderate** or **High**, the exercises and activities that follow are designed to help you to connect even more spiritually with other people.

HONESTY

Honesty is telling the truth – being completely truthful and trustworthy. To be honest with others, you must first be completely honest with yourself. It is telling the whole truth or the whole story. It is not withholding a portion of the truth, giving a false impression or allowing yourself a lie of omission (remaining silent when ethical behavior calls for one to speak up or to tell the whole story). It is an important element of one's character. Honesty gives security and confidence to those with whom you have a personal or working relationship. Truth is the foundation of principle and integrity. It is the primary need of any person who wants meaningful relationships.

In the left-hand column, list the people with whom you can be completely honest.
In the right-hand column, note why you feel this way.

People With Whom I Can Be Honest and My Relationship to Them	Reason(s) I Feel This Way
(Ex. Jack, my friend)	(Ex. He is non-judgmental, honest and always there for me)

HONESTY *(continued)*

In the left-hand column, list the people with whom you *cannot* be honest.
In the right-hand column, note why you feel this way.

People With Whom I Cannot Be Honest and My Relationship to Them	Reason(s) I Feel This Way
(Ex. Jane, my wife)	*(Ex. She finds fault with everything I do and does not understand me)*

© 2010 WHOLE PERSON ASSOCIATES, 101 WEST 2ND ST., SUITE 203, DULUTH MN 55802 ▪ 800-247-6789

Honesty and Trust

Trust is the feeling of confidence and the ability to rely on the honesty, integrity, character and strength of another person or of yourself. This trust comes from your feelings and experiences.

Whom do you trust more than anyone in this world?

_____

What has this person done to earn your trust?

_____

_____

_____

— —

Whom have you trusted, who let you down and didn't live up to your trust? Explain.

_____

_____

What did you learn from that experience?

_____

_____

— —

Who trusts you completely?

_____

Is that trust justified? Have you lived up to that trust?

_____

_____

_____

At any point did you let that person down?

_____

_____

Being Honest with – and Trusting – Yourself

Honesty is one of the primary ways to ensure that you continue on your spiritual path. When most people think of honesty, they think of being honest with other people, however, honesty applies to yourself as well as to other people. Let honesty begin with you. Being honest about your feelings, being trustworthy, and being sincere are ways in which you can be honest with yourself. Self-honesty is about being willing to face yourself with absolute candor and not hold back. In the following table, describe ways (in the various areas of your life) that you are honest and can trust yourself.

Areas of My Life	How I Trust Myself	How I Do Not Trust Myself
Relationship with my partner	Ex: I tell the truth about how I spend money.	Ex: I have a difficult time keeping a budget and documenting the household budget.
Work		
Relationship with my children		
Family		
Community		
Religion and Spirituality		
Other		

What have you concluded – can you trust yourself to be everything you want to be? Write about it.

_____

_____

_____

Honesty Quotations

Pick one of the quotes below, check it, and write below your thoughts, or perhaps an example you have from your life, about that quotation.

- *Who lies for you will lie against you.* ~ **Bosnian Proverb**

- *No person has a good enough memory to make a successful liar.* ~ **Abraham Lincoln**

- *A half truth is a whole lie.* ~ **Yiddish Proverb**

- *Honesty is the cornerstone of all success, without which confidence and ability to perform shall cease to exist.* ~ **Mary Kay Ash**

- *We tell lies when we are afraid . . . afraid of what we don't know, afraid of what others will think, afraid of what will be found out about us. But every time we tell a lie, the thing that we fear grows stronger.* ~ Tad Williams

- *Level with your child by being honest. Nobody spots a phony quicker than a child.* ~ **Mary MacCracken**

- *Honesty is the first chapter of the book of wisdom.* ~ **Thomas Jefferson**

- *The truth needs so little rehearsal.* ~ **Barbara Kingsolver**

_____

_____

_____

_____

_____

_____

_____

_____

_____

_____

_____

_____

Integrity

Integrity is being honest with yourself. It is doing what you say you are going to do, believing in what you say you believe in, and being sure that your actions are the same as your beliefs and values. It is making decisions about what is right and wrong for you and sticking to those decisions as basic elements of your personal code of conduct. It is adhering to your own moral convictions as you respond to every situation with respect for others. It is meeting your obligations in ways that you know are right. It is respecting yourself and keeping your word. It is a value that guarantees all of your other values. It is a foundation of character. When you possess a high level of integrity you can look at yourself in the mirror and feel proud that you are living your life in a moral and ethical way.

Things I think are OKAY
Ex. Humans treating animals as living beings

Things I think are NOT OKAY
Ex. Dog fights, rodeos, abusing animals

When does your conscience bother you? Why?

_____

_____

How do you distinguish what is OKAY for you and what is NOT OKAY for you?

_____

_____

What situations or people have helped you to make these distinctions? In what ways?

_____

_____

_____

Integrity *(continued)*

List some times when you learned a valuable lesson from something that happened to you.

What happened to me	What I learned from it
Ex. I made a promise to a friend and didn't keep it. She never trusted me again.	*Ex. Lying leads to a loss of trust.*

What do you consider to be a moral life?

_____

_____

_____

_____

Integrity Quotations

Check off the quotes about integrity that 'speak to you.'

- *Integrity is the essence of everything successful.* ~ **Richard Buckminster Fuller**

- *Integrity is telling myself the truth. And honesty is telling the truth to other people.* ~ **Spencer Johnson**

- *My grandfather once told me that there are two kinds of people: those who work and those who take credit. He told me to try to be in the first group; there was less competition there.* ~ **Indira Ghandi**

- *Life does not have meaning through mere existence or acquisition or fun. The meaning of life is inherent in the connections we make through honor and obligation.* ~ **Laura Schlessinger**

- *Your reputation and integrity are everything. Follow through on what you say you're going to do. Your credibility can only be built over time, and it is built from the history of your words and actions.* ~ **Maria Razumich-Zec**

- *A single lie destroys a whole reputation of integrity.* ~ **Baltasar Gracian**

- *A life lived with integrity – even if it lacks the trappings of fame and fortune is a shining star in whose light others may follow in the years to come.* ~ **Denis Waitley**

- *If you have integrity – nothing else matters. If you don't have integrity – nothing else matters.* ~ **Evelle J. Younger**

Which of the quotes above would you like to have as your personal motto - one that would sound like you – to yourself and to others. Write it here.

_____

_____

_____

_____

Does it sound like you now? If not, how can you make an effort (and perhaps a commitment) to strive to work on your values, integrity, honesty, compassion and humility – to live up to that motto?

_____

_____

_____

_____

Humility

Humility is being free of pride and arrogance. It is being modest about your self-worth, acknowledging your talents and strengths, and being willing to accept that things may be different from the way you think they are. It is giving credit to others for their ideas or accomplishments rather than taking all of the credit for yourself. It is seeing every moment as an opportunity to learn and to welcome the input of others in order to be a better person or act in a better way.

In the following table, list people you like to impress and why.

People I Like to Impress	Why I Try to Impress Them
Ex. My very well-educated friend	Ex. I want to seem as smart as she is. I feel insecure.

Humility Quotes

Check off the quotations that you feel relate to you.
If they relate to someone you know, write the person's name underneath the quote.

- *Some people are born on third base and go through life thinking they hit a triple.*
  ~ Barry Switzer

- *When someone sings his own praises, he always gets the tune too high.*
  ~ Mary H. Waldrip

- *None are so empty as those who are full of themselves.* **~ Benjamin Whichcote**

- *Looking at yourself in the mirror isn't exactly a study of life.* **~ Lauren Bacall**

- *Humility is like underwear, essential, but indecent if it shows.* **~ Helen Nielsen**

- *You shouldn't gloat about anything you've done; you ought to keep going and find something better to do.* **~ David Packard**

- *Nobody stands taller than those willing to stand corrected.* **~ William Safire**

- *Modesty is the art of encouraging people to find out for themselves how wonderful you are.* **~ Source Unknown**

Write about your favorite quotation above and your thoughts and feelings about it.

Author:_____

My thoughts and feelings:_____

_____

_____

_____

_____

_____

_____

_____

_____

Compassion

Compassion is an emotion that emerges from observing someone's pain and your active desire to help and to alleviate his suffering. It is best described by the Golden Rule, "Do unto others as you would have them do unto you." In many of the major religious traditions it is considered to be the greatest of virtues. Compassion is a quality that needs to be extended to oneself. Having compassion for yourself means that you honor and accept your humanness. It is often a lack of love for ourselves that inhibits our compassion toward others. If we make friends with ourselves, then there is no obstacle to opening our hearts and minds to others.

In the following table, identify the people for whom you feel compassion and why.

People for Whom I Feel Compassion	Why I Feel Compassion for Them
Ex. The homeless	Ex. I feel like they are invisible to most of society. I believe they are good people who need compassion from others and some good breaks.

Compassion – Giving Back

Many people on a spiritual path feel called upon to volunteer and/or to give back. Volunteering is usually the outcome of compassion and it can include time spent helping other people or creatures working in an animal shelter, working with a non-profit that helps needy or under-privileged children, or working with a large national or international non-profit organization.

On the lines that follow, list some of the ways you would like to volunteer or give back, now or in the future.

_____   _____

_____   _____

_____   _____

_____   _____

_____   _____

_____   _____

_____   _____

Here are a few quotations to think about:

- *Compassion is that which makes the heart of the good move at the pain of others. It crushes and destroys the pain of others; thus, it is called compassion. It is called compassion because it shelters and embraces the distressed.* ~ **The Buddha**

- *Bundelkhand has animal shelters run by Jains. Jain monks go to inordinate lengths to avoid killing any living creature, sweeping the ground in front of them in order to avoid killing insects, and even wearing a face mask to avoid inhaling the smallest fly.* ~ **Anonymous**

- *My experience is that people who have been through painful, difficult times are filled with compassion.* ~ **Amy Grant**

- *Compassion is a foundation for sharing our aliveness and building a more humane world.* ~ **Martin Lowenthal**

- *Some people are filled by compassion and a desire to do good, and simply don't think anything's going to make a difference.* ~ **Meryl Streep**

Check the quotation you liked best.

Gratitude

Gratitude is very important as you travel on your spiritual journey. Gratitude is a positive attitude in acknowledgement of something you have already received or will receive in the future. People who are grateful experience higher levels of well-being and life satisfaction, and they are more content in their relationships with other people. They count their blessings every day.

PEOPLE in my life and why I am grateful for them
Ex. I am grateful for my brother. He has always been someone I could talk to and count on.

THINGS in my life and why I am grateful for them
Ex. I am grateful that I live in a sturdy house and am protected from the bad weather.

Gratitude Quotations

- *If the only prayer you would say in your whole life is "thank you" that would suffice.*
  ~ Meister Eckhart

- *Can you see the holiness in those things you take for granted – a paved road or a washing machine? If you concentrate on finding what is good in every situation, you will discover that your life will suddenly be filled with gratitude, a feeling that nurtures the soul.* ~ Rabbi Harold Kushner

- *As each day comes to us refreshed and anew, so does my gratitude renew itself daily. The breaking of the sun over the horizon is my grateful heart dawning upon a blessed world.* **~ Adabella Radici**

- *As we express our gratitude, we must never forget that the highest appreciation is not to utter words, but to live by them.* **~ John Fitzgerald Kennedy**

- *We often take for granted the very thing that most deserves our gratitude.*
  ~ Cynthis Ozick

- *Let us rise up and be thankful, for if we didn't learn a lot today, at least we learned a little, and if we didn't learn a little, at least we didn't get sick, and if we got sick, at least we didn't die; so, let us all be thankful.* **~ Buddha**

- *You say grace before meals. All right. But I say grace before the concert and the opera, and grace before the play and pantomime, and grace before I open a book, and grace before sketching, painting, swimming, fencing, boxing, walking, playing, dancing and grace before I dip the pen in the ink.* **~ G. K. Chesterton**

- *Gratitude unlocks the fullness of life. It turns what we have into enough, and more. It turns denial into acceptance, chaos into order, confusion into clarity . . . It turns problems into gifts, failures into success, the unexpected into perfect timing and mistakes into important events. Gratitude makes sense of our past, brings peace for today and creates a vision for tomorrow.* **~ Melodie Beattie**

Which is your favorite? Why?

_____

_____

_____

_____

_____

Connecting with Others

How would you describe your most effective ways of connecting with other people?
Ex. Volunteering together, sharing information about causes or similar interests.

_____

_____

_____

_____

What do you feel you gain by these connections with others?
Ex. Having someone who supports my interests whom I can trust.

_____

_____

_____

_____

How would you describe your least effective ways of connecting with other people?
Ex. Telephoning regularly, meeting often, listening with intent

_____

_____

_____

_____

What do you feel you lose by this lack of connection?
Ex. A closer friendship, not having some people in my life when I need their support.

_____

_____

_____

_____

Personal Excuses to Avoid Giving Back to the Universe

- "I can't empathize with the person(s)."

- "I don't get excited about helping others."

- "I do not have feelings of guilt when I do not help others."

- "I don't have time."

- "I have not been trained to volunteer."

- "I have to attend to my own needs first."

- "I'm not a counselor."

- "I've never helped in the past."

- "People don't want or appreciate help."

- "What do I get out of it?"

The Spiritual Connection

One aspect of connection leads to another.

- When you speak the truth, you build your sense of honesty

- As your honesty builds, you develop integrity

- As your integrity builds, you feel less of a need to impress others, so you develop humility

- As you become more humble, you feel gratitude for everything and everyone in your life.

- As you develop gratitude you become compassionate and interested in being helpful to other people.

SECTION III:
Spiritual Living Scale

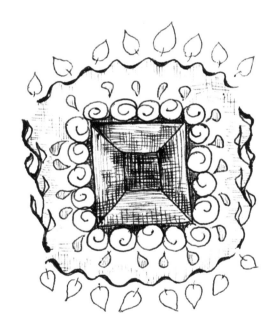

NAME _____   DATE _____

Spiritual Living Scale Directions

The Spiritual Living Scale is designed to help you assess if and how you tap into your spirituality and integrate spiritual themes into your daily life. This assessment contains 36 statements. Read each of the statements and decide if the statement is true or false for you. If it is true, circle the word **TRUE** next to the statement. If the statement is false, circle the word **FALSE** next to the statement. Ignore the letters after the **TRUE** and **FALSE** choices. They are for scoring purposes and will be used later. Complete all 36 items before going back to score the assessment.

In the following example, the circled False indicates that the item is false for the person completing the assessment:

1. I am aware of my natural strengths and weaknesses   True (A)   False (B)

This is not a test and there are no right or wrong answers. Do not spend too much time thinking about your answers. Your initial response will likely be the most true for you. Be sure to respond to every statement.

(Turn to the next page and begin)

Spiritual Living Scale

1. I am aware of my natural strengths and weaknesses . . . . True (A)   False (B)

2. I understand my special purpose. . . . . True (A)   False (B)

3. I think I respond to negative events in my life according to
   my own personal code of values . . . . True (A)   False (B)

4. I worry too much about things . . . . True (B)   False (A)

5. I flow with the natural currents of life . . . . True (A)   False (B)

6. I rarely take time for the small pleasures in life . . . . True (B)   False (A)

TOTAL = _____

7. I have trouble thinking creatively. . . . . True (B)   False (A)

8. I have fun playing with ideas . . . . True (A)   False (B)

9. I am able to see the big picture right away . . . . True (A)   False (B)

10. Because I follow convention, I am not as successful
    as I could be. . . . . True (B)   False (A)

11. I look for different ways to do things and don't mind
    being a non-conformist . . . . True (A)   False (B)

12. I can visualize and see mental pictures . . . . True (A)   False (B)

TOTAL = _____

13. I do not have many hobbies or interests . . . . True (B)   False (A)

14. I put aside time to be playful and silly. . . . . True (A)   False (B)

15. I rarely experience playful moments . . . . True (B)   False (A)

16. I enjoy being childlike . . . . True (A)   False (B)

17. I try to have fun at whatever I do. . . . . True (A)   False (B

18. Others say I am fun to be around . . . . True (A)   False (B)

TOTAL = _____

(Continued on the next page)

(Spiritual Living Scale continued)

19. I see most situations in a positive light . . . . True (A)   False (B)

20. I am content with whatever life throws my way . . . . True (A)   False (B)

21. I do not feel I have enough to be happy . . . . True (B)   False (A

22. I look for the good in everything and everyone. . . . . True (A)   False (B)

23. I am pleased with my life in general . . . . True (A)   False (B)

24. I am not optimistic about my future . . . . True (B)   False (A)

TOTAL = _____

25. I am unable to live in the moment. . . . . True (B)   False (A)

26. I feel anxious without a plan . . . . True (B)   False (A)

27. I do things on the spur of the moment . . . . True (A)   False (B)

28. My current lifestyle does not support my going with the flow. . . . . . True (B)   False (A)

29. I am curious and like to try new things . . . . True (A)   False (B)

30. I like to be spontaneous in life. . . . . True (A)   False (B)

TOTAL = _____

31. I have a good sense of humor . . . . True (A)   False (B)

32. I am willing to laugh at myself. . . . . True (A)   False (B)

33. I use my sense of humor to cope with challenges . . . . True (A)   False (B)

34. My sense of humor has helped me develop humility. . . . . True (A)   False (B)

35. I like to laugh at others . . . . True (B)   False (A)

36. I use humor to help me get through a tough situation . . . . True (A)   False (B)

TOTAL = _____

(Go to the Scoring Directions on the next page)

Spiritual Living Scale Scoring Directions

The Spiritual Living Scale is designed to measure if and how you have been able to integrate spiritual themes into your life.

To score the Spiritual Living Scale focus on the "A" and "B" after each choice rather than the **TRUE** or **FALSE**. For each section, count the number of answers you circled with an "A" next to it. Put that number in the **TOTAL** line at the end of each of the six sections. Transfer your scores to the lines below:

Section 1 (Questions 1 – 6)   = _____ (Self-Awareness)

Section 2 (Questions 7 – 12)   = _____ (Creativity)

Section 3 (Questions 13 – 18)   = _____ (Playfulness)

Section 4 (Questions 19 – 24)   = _____ (Optimism)

Section 5 (Questions 25 – 30)   = _____ (Flow)

Section 6 (Questions 31 – 36)   = _____ (Humor)

Now, total all of your above scores to get your Grand Total.
Put that number on the Spiritual Living Grand Total below.

Spiritual Living Grand Total   = _____

Profile Interpretation

TOTAL SCALES SCORES	RESULT	INDICATIONS
Scores of 5 or 6 or a Grand Total from 25 to 36	High	You possess and integrate into your life many of the characteristics important in living a spiritually-effective life. You will enjoy the following exercises.
Scores of 3 or 4 or a Grand Total from 13 to 24	Moderate	You possess and integrate into your life some of the characteristics important in living a spiritually-effective life. The exercises that follow will help you to develop a more spiritually-oriented life.
Scores of 0 to 2 or a Grand Total from 0 to 12	Low	You do not seem to possess and rarely integrate into your life many of the characteristics important in living a spiritually-effective life. The exercises that follow will be help you to explore how you can begin to live a more spiritual life.

The higher your score on the scales of this assessment, the more your life already leans toward a spiritual path. In the areas in which you score in the **Moderate** or **Low** range, making an effort to improve on them will lead to feeling more spiritual. No matter if you scored **Low**, **Moderate** or **High**, the exercises and activities that follow are designed to help you to begin, or continue, your spiritual path.

Self-Awareness – Scale Description

People on a spiritual path have self-awareness and self-knowledge about their bodies, minds, talents and spiritual gifts. It allows them to cultivate self-respect and develop a firm grip on reality. One tool is acknowledging your strengths and learning to use them effectively, as well as working on your weaknesses. List them below.

MY STRENGTHS
Ex. Compassion

MY WEAKNESSES
Ex. Overly trusting

My gifts that might lean toward a spiritual path are . . .

_____

_____

_____

I am most proud of . . .

_____

_____

Others say I am . . .

_____

_____

Creativity – Scale Description

People whose lives lean toward spirituality tend to be able to think and express themselves creatively. They are able to express themselves in many different ways. They enjoy playing with ideas and identifying different ways to do things. They are imaginative and able to visualize a variety of mental pictures. Creative people tend to express themselves through writing, art, music, photography, sewing, etc. As they allow themselves to participate in creative activities, they feel more nurtured and connected.

"The creative is the place where no one else has ever been. You have to leave the city of your comfort and go into the wilderness of your intuition. What you'll discover will be wonderful. What you'll discover is yourself." ~ **Alan Alda**

Have you ever left 'the city of your comfort'? Tell us about it.

_____

_____

_____

_____

What are some new ways you would like to play with some creative ideas you have seen in your mind's eye?

_____

_____

_____

How can you go about it?

_____

_____

_____

_____

Playfulness – Scale Description

People who are on a spiritual path tend to be playful. Playfulness does not refer to any particular type of activity but can take many forms depending on each person. People can love their work, but also can find meaning and fulfillment by engaging in playful activities. They experience many childlike moments of awe and wonder in their lives.

The Types of Activities That Help Me Feel Playful

Activity Types	Activities Through Which I Feel Playful
Creative	*(Ex. Painting)*
Physical	*(Ex. Badminton)*
Intellectual	*(Ex. Interactive classes)*
Social	*(Ex. A costume party)*
Spiritual	*(Ex. Walking a dog)*
Leadership	*(Ex. Team activities)*
Analytical	*(Ex. Computer games)*

Optimism – Scale Description

Some people find spiritual meaning in the path of optimism. It is a journey of trying to see things on the bright side. Despite disappointments and challenges, they are usually able to view the possibilities of the future and become confident in their ability to accomplish or re-establish their goals and find happiness.

Complete the tables below. These could be from any facet of your life: work, family, events, country, politics, etc.

Things I am optimistic about

Ex. My children

_____   _____

_____   _____

_____   _____

_____   _____

_____   _____

Things I am pessimistic about

Ex. My job

_____   _____

_____   _____

_____   _____

_____   _____

_____   _____

What situations in particular do you think about in a pessimistic way?

_____

_____

How can you use optimism to help you when you are feeling hopeless?

_____

_____

Optimistic and Pessimistic People

Complete the tables below. These could be family members, friends, community members, relatives, TV, movie or book characters, etc.

Optimistic People

Ex. Mary Poppins

_____   _____

_____   _____

_____   _____

_____   _____

Pessimistic People

Ex. Robert in "Everybody Loves Raymond"

_____   _____

_____   _____

_____   _____

_____   _____

Becoming More Optimistic

You can learn to be more optimistic by being aware of your thoughts and patterns and by learning to reframe your thoughts in a positive light. Try this simple exercise the next time you begin to think pessimistically.

Write a situation about which you tend to be pessimistic. *(Ex. A new task at work)*

_____

_____

When this happens, what are your first thoughts? *(Ex. I HATE my boss)*

_____

_____

Now reframe the negative thoughts for positive thoughts. *(Ex. this may be an opportunity to find better work or something that suits me better)*

_____

_____

Flow – Scale Description

People on a spiritual path are usually able to "go-with-the-flow." They live in the moment and find contentment and happiness. They don't wait for tomorrow or until they will accomplish something in the future. They explore life and want to experience all they can. They are aware of the activities that bring them a sense of flow.

Experiencing Flow

People have experienced moments when they feel in the flow of life and feel more spiritually alive. Whether it is while taking a walk in nature, playing in a soccer game or traveling, people experience those spiritual moments when all time seems to stop and they feel at one with the universe. It is important that you explore those activities that bring you a feeling of wellness and enhance your overall well-being.

Going with the flow moment	How I feel when I am "In-the-Flow"
(Ex. Saying "YES" to going on a spontaneous walk)	*(Ex. Calm, soothed, ready to get back to my chores or work)*

Humor – Scale Description

People on a spiritual path usually use humor to enhance their spirituality. They believe that humor is critical in facing challenges in life and that a sense of humor can provide them with perspective. They use humor to cope with stress and stay focused on what is important. They are able to laugh at themselves and the absurdities of life, making them more fully human. As adults we need to maintain our childlike nature and ability to laugh.

What causes you to laugh? (TV shows, people, things you read or that tickle your funny bone)

_____

_____

_____

If you no longer laugh very much, when did that happen? What caused this?

_____

_____

_____

What can you do to bring more laughter into your life?

_____

_____

_____

In what types of life challenges have you used laughter and/or humor to help you overcome and/or heal?

_____

_____

_____

How do you think humor enhances your health and well-being?

_____

_____

_____

"Laughter is internal jogging." ~ **Norman Cousins**

Spiritual Living

What has occurred in your life that has prevented or distracted you from beginning or continuing on a spiritual path?

_____

_____

_____

_____

_____

_____

What can you now do to overcome these hurdles?

_____

_____

_____

_____

_____

_____

What techniques in this chapter can help you begin or continue on your spiritual path?

_____

_____

_____

_____

_____

_____

Your Connection

Think of a time in your life when you felt a shift, and you felt more connected to yourself and/or the universe? Explain.

_____

_____

_____

_____

_____

_____

_____

_____

Where are you when you feel your inner peace or a connection to the universe? Describe the place and how you feel.

_____

_____

_____

_____

_____

_____

_____

_____

_____

_____

People Who Live a Spiritual Life . . .

- are spontaneous and live in each moment.

- seek to change the world by changing themselves first.

- rely on intuition for inner guidance.

- trust that challenges are beneficial lessons to be learned.

- seek to balance the inner spiritual world and outer every day living.

- believe that they are spiritual beings who have human experiences, rather than human beings who have spiritual experiences.

- experience purpose and meaning in their life.

- look outside of themselves for love, support and strength when needed.

The Nature of Spirituality

Reflect on the following questions:

- What if the world is a school for learning and growth?

- Why are meaningful activities different for different people?

- How is a person's success measured?

- What if people could love everyone, not just certain people?

- What if simplicity and peacefulness were achieved by all people?

- Are there miracles? What has happened in your life that could come close to what you would call a miracle?

84

SECTION IV:
Personal Centering Scale

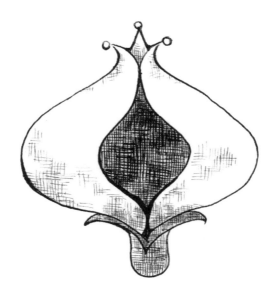

NAME _____ DATE _____

Personal Centering Scale Directions

Many paths to spirituality may be open to you and you will also discover several spiritual disciplines that can help you deepen your spiritual growth and center you. **Personal centering refers to tuning into, or coming into, greater harmony with your inner natural self.** This assessment will help you identify the ways to embark on a spiritual path, identify the pathways you are already following to enhance your spiritual growth, and perhaps give you some tips about other resources. Read each statement carefully. Circle the number of the response that shows how descriptive each statement is of you. Use the following scale:

4 = Always or Frequently   3 = Often   2 = Sometimes   1 = Rarely, if Ever

I like to pray or meditate . . .

  1. when I feel stressed 4   (3)   2   1

In the above example, the circled 3 indicates that the test taker likes to pray or meditate often when stressed.

This is not a test and there are no right or wrong answers. Do not spend too much time thinking about your answers. Your initial response will likely be the most true for you. Be sure to respond to every statement.

(Turn to the next page and begin)

Personal Centering Scale

Please respond to each of the statements by circling the response which best describes you.

4 = Always or Frequently   3 = Often   2 = Sometimes   1 = Rarely, if Ever

I like to pray or meditate . . .

1. when I feel stressed	4	3	2	1
2. to help me feel connected	4	3	2	1
3. to tune into my inner voice	4	3	2	1
4. regularly if possible	4	3	2	1
5. to ask for guidance	4	3	2	1
6. for health benefits	4	3	2	1
7. so I can be kinder to other people	4	3	2	1
8. to get rid of my anger and negativity	4	3	2	1

Meditation/Prayer = _____

On the topic of religion . . .

9. I have an active religious faith	4	3	2	1
10. I am strongly affiliated with a house of worship	4	3	2	1
11. my faith helps me cope with everyday challenges	4	3	2	1
12. I attend a house of worship regularly	4	3	2	1
13. I find hope and meaning through my faith	4	3	2	1
14. my faith provides me with a sense of spiritual well-being	4	3	2	1
15. I participate actively in functions of a house of worship	4	3	2	1
16. I feel supported by members of my religious affiliation	4	3	2	1

Religion = _____

(Continued on the next page)

(Personal Centering Scale *continued*)

Please respond to each of the statements by circling the response which best describes you.

4 = Always or Frequently   3 = Often   2 = Sometimes   1 = Rarely, if Ever

To feel connected to nature, I . . .

17. garden and help plants grow.	4	3	2	1
18. care for animals with love.	4	3	2	1
19. work towards a "greener" society	4	3	2	1
20. attend an outdoor retreat	4	3	2	1
21. camp or hike.	4	3	2	1
22. try to conserve the earth's resources	4	3	2	1
23. spend time outdoors	4	3	2	1
24. experience the joy and beauty of scenery	4	3	2	1

Nature = _____

I read and contemplate spiritual messages . . .

25. to help me choose what is best to do or not do	4	3	2	1
26. to enhance my spiritual progress	4	3	2	1
27. to provide me with greater meaning in my life.	4	3	2	1
28. to help me live my life better	4	3	2	1
29. to help nurture me and make me feel safer	4	3	2	1
30. to provide me with concepts to better understand life.	4	3	2	1
31. to provide me with greater wisdom	4	3	2	1
32. to answer my questions	4	3	2	1

Spiritual Messages = _____

(Continued on the next page)

(Personal Centering Scale *continued***)**

Please respond to each of the statements by circling the response which best describes you:

4 = Always or Frequently   3 = Often   2 = Sometimes   1 = Rarely, if Ever

I use body-mind centered techniques (stretching, yoga, tai chi, Qi Gong, etc.) because they help me . . .

33. maintain a well-toned body	4	3	2	1
34. raise my self-awareness	4	3	2	1
35. quiet the internal chatter of my mind	4	3	2	1
36. channel the energy in my body	4	3	2	1
37. integrate meditation and movement	4	3	2	1
38. feel more connected to the universe.	4	3	2	1
39. heighten my spirituality	4	3	2	1
40. feel more patient and relaxed	4	3	2	1

Body-Mind Centered Techniques = _____

Regarding the sacred in my life, I . . .

41. recognize the sacred in myself through my intuition	4	3	2	1
42. go to a place that feels sacred to me	4	3	2	1
43. recognize the sacred in other people intuitively.	4	3	2	1
44. feel connected	4	3	2	1
45. am open to and intuitively sense everyday miracles	4	3	2	1
46. feel a sense of awe in my life...	4	3	2	1
47. experience moments when a mundane experience becomes inspiring.	4	3	2	1
48. retreat to a sacred place to connect with my inner self	4	3	2	1

Sacred Experiences = _____

(Go to the Scoring Directions on the next page)

Personal Centering Scale Scoring Directions

The assessment you just completed is designed to help you explore how involved you are in activities designed to help center yourself, become more aware of others, and learn more effective ways of practicing and benefiting from these disciplines. For each of the sections on the previous pages, add the scores you circled for each of the sections. Put the total on the line marked with the Topic name at the end of each section.

Then, transfer your totals to the spaces below:

TOTALS   **TOPIC NAME**

_____ Meditation/Prayer Scale

_____ Religion Scale

_____ Nature Scale

_____ Spiritual Messages Scale

_____ Body-Mind Centered Techniques Scale

_____ Sacred Experiences Scale

After you have completed transferring your total scores, look at the Profile Interpretation section below for more information about your scores on the assessment. Scale descriptions have been provided on the next page, as well as information and exercises to help you to use your body and mind as a way of beginning or continuing on your spiritual path, on the following pages.

Profile Interpretation

TOTAL SCALES SCORES	RESULT	INDICATIONS
Scores from 25 to 32	High	You have been practicing these disciplines which could enhance your spiritual growth.
Scores from 16 to 24	Moderate	You have been practicing some of these disciplines.
Scores from 8 to 15	Low	You may not have been practicing many of these disciplines but this is a perfect time to start.

Scale Descriptions

1. Meditation/Prayer

People scoring high on this scale might find their spirituality through a form of meditation or prayer.

>You probably pray or meditate to have more quiet time, reflection and inner peace.

2. Religion

People scoring high on this scale might find their spirituality through religious practice, but not necessarily.

>You probably belong to an organized group that acts with a mission and intention of presenting specific doctrines and teachings as a way to live your life.

3. Nature

People scoring high on this scale might find their spirituality through being part of nature and spending time in natural surroundings.

>You probably enjoy such activities as bird watching, horseback riding, gardening, caring for animals, farming, camping, hiking and taking nature walks.

4. Spiritual Messages

People scoring high on this scale find their spirituality through inspiring books or quotations of spiritual leaders, and connecting with other spiritual seekers.

>You probably look to these messages and relationships to nurture yourself, understand the meaning of life and death better and help yourself to live more fully.

5. Body-Mind Centered Techniques

People scoring high on this scale might find their spirituality by engaging in physical activities that help them to remain calm and focused, relieve stress, strengthen the body's energy and reach greater spiritual heights.

>You probably enjoy such activities as running in marathons, martial arts, yoga, mountain climbing, exercising and Tai Chi.

6. Sacred Experiences

People scoring high on this scale are intuitively able to see the sacred in the universe, in others, in their own experiences and in themselves.

>You probably begin to see the sacred within yourself and in the world through small everyday miracles like the beauty of a sunset, the touch of another person or in the awesomeness of nature. For you, your life feels sacred.

The following exercises will provide you with information and activities to help deepen your spiritual growth and center you. Start with the activities that provide you with the most meaning and growth, and then expand your repertoire of activities.

Meditation and Prayer

Meditation and prayer are two ways in which people experience a union with their spirituality. One way to think of these two disciplines is as complementary components on a spiritual journey. Through meditation, you are able to clear the clutter of restless thoughts, and you are ready to connect to your inner self.

MEDITATION quiets your usually busy mind and allows you to be in the present. Through the mental and physical stilling of your mind, you will be able to achieve a heightened degree of mental clarity. The basics of meditation include sitting quietly, closing your eyes and focusing your mind inward by paying attention to the flow of your breath. The natural rhythms of your breathing will keep your mind from focusing on other things. If you do have thoughts while you are concentrating on your breath, notice them and let them float on by. You should begin your meditation practice slowly, maybe five minutes a day and then gradually extend your minutes until you reach a comfortable time.

Write about experiences you have had with meditation before.

_____

_____

If you do not meditate regularly, have you ever tried it? Would you consider trying it now? Why or why not?

_____

_____

PRAYER is communicating with a belief in a higher power. While the methods of prayer may vary, the intentions are the same — to give praise, thanks, or to ask for guidance, wishes or help.

One may engage in prayer in public as a part of a group or in private. Words used in prayer can be written in a prayer book or words straight from your heart and mind. Prayer can be said aloud, silently or expressed through music.

Prayer is conscious and intentional. Each person's prayer is unique, individual and personal and can be done regularly or as needed.

If you pray, when do you pray? How do you pray?

_____

_____

How do you feel comforted after praying?

_____

_____

Spirituality and Religion

At times in history, the terms *spiritual* and *religious* were explained as one and the same concept, but not anymore. More recently, religion has been described as a repetitive faith practice, a membership in a religious institution and participation in that institution's formal rituals, the study and practice of the official doctrines and readings or following the traditions of the religion. Some people connect their religion and spirituality and some do not.

In general, what are your thoughts and feelings about spirituality?

_____

_____

_____

_____

_____

In general, what are your thoughts and feelings about religion?

_____

_____

_____

_____

_____

What comments might you have about a connection between religion and spirituality?

_____

_____

_____

_____

_____

Nature

Being connected to nature can enhance your spirituality. For some people, taking a walk in the woods, standing beside a flowing river or standing on a mountain overlooking a lake can be a spiritual experience. For these people, being actively involved in the joy and awe provided by nature expands their vision and provides them with a deeper sense of themselves.

By using nature as a spiritual discipline, you are accepting that everything in the world is a living, conscious and interconnected system that must be experienced. People who connect nature with spirituality love to experience the wonders of the world and nature in detail. Nature enhances their sense of spirituality. Some people enjoy nature-based activities simply as a leisure-time activity. For these people, nature provides them with activities that they can enjoy even though they may not identify this enjoyment or pleasure as a spiritual experience. Describe in the spaces that follow how you view the connection between yourself and nature.

Describe your reaction to the statement that all stones, people, trees, plants, animals, clouds, stars (and many other things) are living conscious beings.

_____

_____

_____

What types of activities do you like to do in a natural setting (hiking, fishing, etc.)?

_____

_____

_____

What is the PERFECT nature setting for you? In what way are you able to be there? When? How often?

_____

_____

_____

What prevents you from spending more time in natural settings?

_____

_____

_____

Describe the way you feel in a natural setting. Would you call this a spiritual feeling?

_____

_____

_____

SECTION IV: ACTIVITY HANDOUTS

Spiritual Messages

More than ever, people are searching for meaning in their lives. Explanations and definitions of spirituality can be found in the wide array of messages from many different spiritual teachers and leaders, stories, quotations, CDs, online sites and other sources of time-proven wisdom. Spiritual messages — your willingness to listen to them, read about them, study them and integrate them into your life — can enhance your self-awareness and assist you along your spiritual path.

What would you like to learn about spirituality?

_____

_____

_____

_____

What/who do you find to be spiritually moving?

_____

_____

_____

_____

Where could you find additional inspiration?

_____

_____

_____

_____

With whom could you have a conversation that would be spirit-filled?

_____

_____

_____

What would you like to gain from the array of spiritual messages available today?

_____

_____

_____

_____

Body-Mind Centered Techniques

When it comes to spiritual disciplines, it is important to remember the union of body and mind as an opportunity for spiritual work. Spiritual traditions have taught methods of using body and mind to enhance your spiritual awareness. Centering techniques can be used alone or along with other spiritual disciplines described in this chapter. Several important body-mind centering techniques are listed here:

Guided Imagery – Guided imagery is a gentle but powerful technique that focuses and directs the imagination. You can invent your own imagery or listen to imagery on CDs. Either way, your own imagination will sooner or later take over. It is a form of deliberate, directed daydreaming, using all the senses, to create an immersive, right-brained experience in which a desired end-state, such as healing, reconciliation, problem solving or acquiring a sense of oneness with the universe can be recalled or imagined.

Yoga – The ultimate purpose of yoga is to unite with the energy that runs through your body. Through yoga, your body can experience higher states of being. Yoga is slow and mindful. It cultivates a relationship between body, mind and spirit and it requires discipline and commitment to receive the benefits. Yoga involves gentle postures and breathing exercises to stimulate the organs and relax the nervous system.

Qigong – Qigong is the practice of movements and meditations that influence the vital force inside the body, known as Qi. Qigong practitioners can absorb and channel the energy of the universe to remain healthy and grow spiritually.

Tai Chi – Tai Chi is a soft, internally focused martial art used for self-defense, self-healing, and spiritual growth and enlightenment. Tai Chi is a traditional set of up to 108 separate movements that are practiced in a definite order. Tai Chi is practiced in slow motion to enable the energy in the body to harmonize with the energy of the universe.

Spiritual Breathing – Spiritual breathing is much more than simply the movement of air in and out of your lungs. It is a practice that enhances your bodily functions and increases your life force. By practicing spiritual breathing, you can relax your mind, calm your emotions and enhance your spiritual awareness.

Chakra Energy Balancing – According to the ancient Hindu texts, Chakras are the seven primary energy centers in the human body. These Chakras are not made of energy, but they are responsible for directing the flow of energy throughout the body. Chakras are located along a running line from the top of the head to the base of the spine, and are very important to physical, mental, and spiritual well-being. When you are experiencing stress, your Chakras can become blocked and out of balance and this can lead to physical illnesses. Although there are many ways of balancing Chakras, the use of sound is an effective way to open the Chakras so that energy flows efficiently throughout the body. Soft music and beautiful sounds have an emotional as well as physical resonance that leads to spiritual well-being.

Now that you are aware of some of these centering techniques, which have you already tried? How were they successful? Which other techniques would you be willing to make a commitment to try?

_____

_____

_____

_____

Practicing Body-Mind Centering Techniques

Are you currently practicing any types of body-mind centered techniques? What are they?

_____

_____

_____

_____

_____

What types of body-mind centered techniques would you like to begin practicing and why?

_____

_____

_____

_____

_____

What might you benefit from them?

_____

_____

_____

_____

_____

Are there other body-mind centered techniques you are attracted to that might help you feel spirit-filled?

_____

_____

_____

_____

_____

SECTION IV: ACTIVITY HANDOUTS

Sacred Experiences

Sacred experiences are feelings like no other. They can occur spontaneously and fill one with wonder and awe. Moments of a sacred experience may feel mystical, glorious, supernatural, unearthly and/or blissful. They can be experiences in which time seems to stand still, or a moment when you are without words, or a flash when you feel as if a miracle has occurred.

Reflect upon a time in your life when you experienced something which you were not able to adequately describe or an experience that just took your breath away. Describe on the lines below.

_____

_____

_____

What experiences have you had when time seemed to stand still?

_____

_____

_____

Describe a time when you experienced something that you felt was a miracle? What happened?

_____

_____

_____

What is your perception of a sacred place?

_____

_____

_____

Describe a sacred place you have created for yourself - a place to just "be."

_____

_____

_____

If you don't have a sacred space, where could you have one? What objects or reminders would you want to include in that space?

_____

_____

_____

The Sacred Experience of Intuition

"The Intuitive mind is a sacred gift . . ." ~ **Albert Einstein**

Intuition describes your way of knowing things without knowing how you know them. Most people spend a great deal of their time in analytical thinking and neglect their intuitive thinking. Thus your intuitive mind is probably less developed than your analytical mind. The good news is that you can develop your intuition more fully. As you begin to feel comfortable with silence and become more mindful and present in the moment, you will begin to access your intuition in a deeper and wiser way of knowing and being.

When you are ready, take the steps to recognize and use your intuition:

- Allow your mind to become quiet, using meditation or one of the other techniques in this chapter.

- Allow yourself to be open to receive intuitive knowledge.

- Develop a non-judgmental attitude that allows your intuition to express itself.

- Trust your intuition.

Intuition is a natural perception we all have deep within us. It is accessed in several ways:

- courage
- images
- symbols
- daydreams
- words entering our minds
- sounds
- touch
- dreams
- a hunch
- 'gut' feelings
- mind pictures or visions

Methods you can use to allow intuition to emerge:

- art
- music
- free association
- visualization
- word concentration
- Intuition journal

Keeping a record and journaling intuitive happenings validates them, and sharing experiences accelerates the development of intuition.

Intuition (or hunch – or 'gut' feeling)

Wisdom is often delivered to you by your inner voice, your intuition.

Have you ever known you were going to get a job? Have you ever known that the person you've just met will be a good friend? Have you ever, after something happened, realized that you knew it would happen? If so, you've experienced an intuitive moment.

In the last year, have you experienced an intuition about anything? What was it?

_____

_____

How did you react to that intuitive wisdom?

_____

_____

Were you pleased that you trusted your intuition?

_____

_____

If you did not react to that intuitive wisdom, why not?

_____

_____

What seemed to hold you back from trusting your intuition?

_____

_____

Read the following quotations and write about one in particular.

You have to leave the city of your comfort and go into the wilderness of your intuition. What you'll discover will be wonderful. What you'll discover is yourself. ~ **Alan Alda**

Intuition is the clear conception of the whole at once. ~ **Johann Kaspar Lavater**

Often you have to rely on intuition. ~ **Bill Gates**

You must train your intuition – you must trust the small voice inside you which tells you exactly what to say, what to decide. ~ **Ingrid Bergman**

_____

_____

_____

_____

My Goals for Personal Centering

Goal setting is a way to organize, motivate and feel a sense of direction and control, to move in a positive direction. Writing the goals is one way to increase the likelihood of following through.

The following chart offers a place for you to set short-term goals (for the next three months) and long-term goals (for the next year) for becoming more centered.

In the table below list your goals in specific, attainable terms in the categories in which you would like to participate.

Ways I Will Center Myself	Short-Term Goals (for the next three months)	Long-Term Goals (for the next year)
Meditation and Prayer	*Ex: I will begin meditating five minutes every day starting tomorrow*	*Ex: I will have increased it to at least a half an hour each day*
Religion		
Nature		
Spiritual Messages		
Body-Centered		
Techniques		
Sacred Experiences		
Other Ways I will Center Myself		

Personal Centering Quotations

Choose two of the quotes below. How does each speak to your feelings about personal centering? Perhaps you will find a quote that you disagree with. Write about it also.

- *Meditation is the tongue of the soul and the language of our spirit.* ~ **Jeremy Taylor**

- *Your prayer can be poetry, and poetry can be your prayer.* ~ **Noelani Day**

- *Everybody needs beauty as well as bread, places to play in and pray in, where nature may heal and give strength to body and soul.* ~ **John Muir**

- *It is a wholesome and necessary thing for us to turn again to the earth and in the contemplation of her beauties to know of wonder and humility.* ~ **Rachel Carson**

- *You have to be able to center yourself, to let all of your emotions go. Don't ever forget that you play with your soul as well as your body.* ~ **Kareem Abdul-Jabbar**

- *Watching birds has become part of my daily meditation affirming my connection to the earth body.* ~ **Carol P. Christ**

- *The highest point a man can obtain is not Knowledge, or Virtue, or Goodness, or Victory, but something even greater, more heroic and more despairing: Sacred Awe!* ~ **Nikos Kazantzakis**

_____

_____

_____

_____

_____

_____

_____

_____

_____

_____

Benefits of Practicing Spiritual Disciplines

- Develop patience

- Enhance greater spiritual well-being

- Expand emotional awareness and availability

- Experience inner peace

- Feel relief from stress

- Increase greater awareness of self

- Open ways to feel and show more compassion

- Reduce acute and chronic pain

- Relax

- Strengthen ability to "go-with-the-flow"

- Worry less about the past and future

© 2010 WHOLE PERSON ASSOCIATES, 101 WEST 2ND ST., SUITE 203, DULUTH MN 55802 ▪ 800-247-6789

Types of Spiritual Retreats

- Couples' retreats

- Emotional catharsis retreats

- Energy work retreats

- Fasting retreats

- Meditation retreats

- Nature retreats

- Parent-child retreats

- Religious retreats

- Silence retreats

- Simplicity and solitude retreats

- Wellness retreats

SECTION V:
Spiritual Awareness Scale

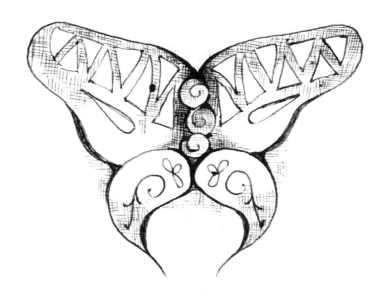

NAME _____ DATE _____

Spiritual Awareness Scale Directions

Life can be very challenging and very satisfying, often at the same time. The essence of spiritual awareness is to better manage the life's challenges and start experiencing the joys that life and the universe has to offer. Spiritual awareness is learning more about yourself, your spiritual nature and ways to open yourself to a spiritual view of life.

The Spiritual Awareness Scale can help you identify the essence of your unique spiritual nature. This assessment contains 28 statements. Read each of the statements and decide how much you agree with the statement. Circle the number of your response on the line to the right of each statement.

In the following example, the circled 1 indicates that the person completing the scale strongly agreed with the statement:

	Strongly Agree	Agree	Disagree	Strongly Disagree
1. I do not have a specific belief system	(1)	2	3	4

This is not a test and there are no right or wrong answers. Do not spend too much time thinking about your answers. Your initial response will likely be the most true for you. Be sure to respond to every statement.

(Turn to the next page and begin)

Spiritual Awareness Scale

	Strongly Agree	Agree	Disagree	Strongly Disagree
1. I do not have a specific belief system	1	2	3	4
2. I like to think deeply about life	4	3	2	1
3. I do things on automatic pilot most of the time	1	2	3	4
4. I can define a purpose for my life	4	3	2	1
5. I cannot speak comfortably about my values	1	2	3	4
6. I rarely contemplate the nature of existence	1	2	3	4
7. I try not to rush through things	4	3	2	1
8. I keep my purpose in mind when I make decisions	4	3	2	1
9. There is a connection between my values and daily activities	4	3	2	1
10. I have often pondered what it means to live an authentic life	4	3	2	1
11. I rarely find myself thinking too deeply about the past or future	4	3	2	1
12. My life is not very meaningful right now	1	2	3	4
13. I continually explore my personal beliefs and values	4	3	2	1
14. I have never thought about the purpose of my existence	1	2	3	4

(Continued on the next page)

(Spiritual Awareness Scale *continued*)

	Strongly Agree	Agree	Disagree	Strongly Disagree
15. I am often not focused on what I am doing	1	2	3	4
16. Meaning in my life helps me deal with stress	4	3	2	1
17. I try to honor other people's beliefs and values	4	3	2	1
18. I have thought about what happens after death	4	3	2	1
19. I rarely find myself "running on automatic"	4	3	2	1
20. I do not search for deeper meanings in my life	1	2	3	4
21. My beliefs and values do not guide my life	1	2	3	4
22. I have many questions about life and existence	4	3	2	1
23. I have a great sense of self-awareness	4	3	2	1
24. My work is not meaningful to me	1	2	3	4
25. I understand why I have my values and beliefs	4	3	2	1
26. I don't care what the meaning of life is	1	2	3	4
27. I find it hard to stay focused on the present	1	2	3	4
28. I look for meaning in the patterns of my life	4	3	2	1

(Go to the Scoring Directions on the next page)

Spiritual Awareness Scale
Scoring Directions

The Spiritual Awareness Scale is designed to measure how consciously you are living your life. Four areas that describe spiritual awareness have been identified in this scale:

- **Values**
- **Self-Exploration**
- **Fully Present**
- **Purpose and Meaning**

The items for each of the four areas are grouped so that you may explore your spiritual awareness.

To score the assessment, look at the items on the previous two pages. Use the spaces below to transfer and record the number which you circled for each individual item. Add the scores for each area.

Values		**Self-Exploration**		**Fully Present**		**Purpose and Meaning**	
Item #	Score	Item #	Score	Item #	Score	Item #	Score
1	_____	2	_____	3	_____	4	_____
5	_____	6	_____	7	_____	8	_____
9	_____	10	_____	11	_____	12	_____
13	_____	14	_____	15	_____	16	_____
17	_____	18	_____	19	_____	20	_____
21	_____	22	_____	23	_____	24	_____
25	_____	26	_____	27	_____	28	_____
Total = _____		Total = _____		Total = _____		Total = _____	

After you have determined your total scores for each area, look at the Profile Interpretation section for more information about your scores on the assessment. Descriptions have been provided, as well as information and exercises to help you to develop or further enhance your spiritual awareness in each of these four areas of spirituality.

(Go to the Profile Interpretation on the next page)

Spiritual Awareness Scale
Profile Interpretation

Find the range for your scores for each scale and use the information below to assist you in the interpretation of your scores.

TOTAL SCALES SCORES	RESULT	INDICATIONS
Scores from 22 to 28	High	You have been able to develop and implement many aspects of personal awareness. The exercises will help you to enhance your spirituality even further.
Scores from 14 to 21	Moderate	You have been able to develop and implement some aspects of personal awareness. The exercises will help you to develop your spirituality even further.
Scores from 7 to 13	Low	You have neither developed nor implemented many aspects of personal awareness. By completing the exercises, you may greatly develop and enhance your spirituality.

(Go to the Scale Descriptions on the next page)

Spiritual Awareness Scale Descriptions

Values

People scoring high in this area have values that guide their decisions, ways they live their lives and the types of activities they enjoy. They possess consistent values that they apply to a variety of situations and decisions in their lives.

Self-Exploration

People scoring high in this area are engaged in a quest for answers to their most interesting questions. They possess a curious nature about their ability to ponder questions of purpose and their place in the overall scheme of things. They grapple with these issues rather than passing over them superficially and mindlessly.

Fully Present

People scoring high in this area tend to be fully present for most of the activities in their lives. Regardless of what they are doing, they stay focused on their task and do not let thoughts of the past or future take them away from being aware of the moment.

Purpose and Meaning

People scoring high in this area have discovered their purpose in life, and that purpose provides them with meaning. They know who they are, why they are here on earth, and who they would like to be. Purpose and meaning provide them with life direction and source of essence.

For any areas in which you scored in the "Low" or "Medium" ranges, find that description on the pages that follow. Read the description and complete the exercises that are included. These exercises will help you to enhance your spiritual awareness.

Your Values

Having consistent values will guide you along your spiritual path. Your values define your character. They impact every part of your life – personal, spiritual, family, career, etc. Values are those guidelines that matter to you as an individual – the ideas and beliefs you hold as special and that must be true for you to live a happy and fulfilled life. Your values begin when you were a child learning from parents and significant adults who influenced your life. Later your values came from peers, social environment and other influences you allowed in your life. Values develop and change. If yours aren't working for you and your life, you have the power to change them. In this sampling of values, place a check *before* each of those that apply to you and add any others that are applicable for you at this time in your life.

__ Abundance	__ Empathy	__ Longevity	__ Sensuality
__ Acceptance	__ Enthusiasm	__ Love	__ Service
__ Accomplishment	__ Family	__ Loyalty	__ Sharing
__ Accuracy	__ Fashion	__ Meticulousness	__ Shrewdness
__ Achievement	__ Financial independence	__ Mindfulness	__ Sincerity
__ Adaptability	__ Flow	__ Modesty	__ Skillfulness
__ Affection	__ Focus	__ Motivation	__ Spirituality
__ Ambition	__ Freedom	__ Neatness	__ Spontaneity
__ Appreciation	__ Friendliness	__ Openness	__ Spunk
__ Assertiveness	__ Frugality	__ Optimism	__ Stability
__ Balance	__ Fun	__ Originality	__ Thankfulness
__ Being the best	__ Giving	__ Passion	__ Thoroughness
__ Belonging	__ Growth	__ Peace	__ Thoughtfulness
__ Benevolence	__ Harmony	__ Presence	__ Tranquility
__ Calmness	__ Heroism	__ Privacy	__ Trust
__ Caring	__ Holiness	__ Proactivity	__ Truth
__ Cheerfulness	__ Honesty	__ Professionalism	__ Uniqueness
__ Compassion	__ Humor	__ Prosperity	__ Warmth
__ Consciousness	__ Independence	__ Punctuality	__ Wisdom
__ Consistency	__ Inquisitiveness	__ Purity	__ Youthfulness
__ Courage	__ Integrity	__ Reasonableness	_____
__ Creativity	__ Intelligence	__ Responsibility	_____
__ Cunning	__ Intuitiveness	__ Religion	_____
__ Daring	__ Justice	__ Resilience	_____
__ Dignity	__ Kindness	__ Respect	_____
__ Diversity	__ Learning	__ Satisfaction	_____
__ Effectiveness	__ Liveliness	__ Self-control	_____
__ Efficiency	__ Logic	__ Self-reliance	_____

Now, put a star *after* those values you would like to develop further.

Values Conflicts

We live in a confusing world, constantly making choices about how we want to live our lives. Ideally, we are making choices based on our belief systems and values. At times, however, we must make decisions that go against our most highly-prized values.

List the ways you are able to live according to your values in a variety of life's situations.

Areas of My Life	Ways I Live According to My Values
Family	
Health	
Friends	
Work	
Leisure time	
Religion	
Material possessions	
Politics	
Other	

Go to the next page for the next step in VALUES CONFLICT.

Values Conflicts (continued)

Note the ways you are not living according to your values in a variety of life situations.

Areas of My Life	Ways I Do Not Live According to My Values
Family	
Health	
Friends	
Work	
Leisure time	
Religion	
Material possessions	
Politics	
Other	

What have you learned from completing this and the previous table?

_____

_____

_____

_____

Self-Exploration

Self-exploration is looking inside yourself, and it is a challenge that takes determination and focus to accomplish. It means becoming aware of what's important to you and understanding yourself, i.e., your values, integrity, goals, dreams, ambitions and purpose in life. Understanding yourself is a lifelong process – and this is a good time to begin.

Who are you?

_____

_____

_____

Who do you want to be?

_____

_____

_____

When you were a child, what or who did you want to be?

_____

_____

_____

What do you want to accomplish?

_____

_____

_____

What adjectives best describe you?

_____

_____

_____

When you daydream, what do you picture yourself doing?

_____

_____

_____

(Continued on the next page)

Self-Exploration *(continued)*

If you had no other obligations or financial issues, how would you spend a month of your time?

_____

_____

_____

What difficult events have made you a stronger person?

_____

_____

_____

In your life to date, what has happened that you are particularly proud of?

_____

_____

_____

Describe the person you want to become.

_____

_____

_____

Five years from now, how would you like to answer this question: "What have I done that I feel the best about?

_____

_____

_____

How do you want to live your life?

_____

_____

_____

What will people say about you after you die?

_____

_____

_____

Fully Present

Awareness, or mindfulness, is about staying fully present – mindful of what you are doing. To be fully present means focusing your attention on the moment. Your body and mind are completely synchronized. It means stopping all the chatter in your head. It means stopping thoughts about what you are going to say next while the other person is talking to you. It means not engaging in one activity and thinking of another. It is standing between the future and past, and precisely in the present moment. Focusing on life's joys and relishing everything you do will help you learn to focus wholeheartedly on whatever task is at hand. Living in the moment means immersing yourself fully in every experience, positive or negative. Slowing down and focusing your awareness will help you stay in the moment.

What types of activities or work do you perform automatically?

_____

_____

_____

What wakes you up from acting so automatically?

_____

_____

_____

What type of activities or work holds your undivided attention and keeps you focused without your even trying?

_____

_____

_____

What people do you feel are "fully present" when they are with you?

_____

_____

_____

How do you feel when another person appears "fully present?"

_____

_____

_____

Staying in the Present

Learning to stay in the present requires several crucial steps. This may sound easy, but will actually take a great deal of practice to master.

The first step to staying in the present is to become more aware of what you are getting caught up in. Are you getting lost in thoughts about the past or future, negative feelings, anxiety, etc.

Example: When walking a dog, you might be thinking about what you need to do for work the next day, worrying about a presentation you have to do, or obsessing about what to have for dinner rather than focusing on walking your pet.

The second step in staying in the present is to switch your entire focus onto what you are doing. Attempt to tune into everything that is happening around you while engaging in the activity.

Example: While walking your pet, you notice the traffic that passes you on the street, the street signs (some you may never have seen before!), the new addition one of your neighbors has put on his house, the redness of the setting sun, the crisp chill in the air that signals fall is coming, the way your pet walks and greets other pets, how fast your heart beats when you walk, the joy your pet experiences during a walk, etc.

As you begin to tune into what is happening around you, you will begin to get out of your mind and into the activity. You will begin to feel more in the present and feel more alive. Remember, being present means you are attending to what is happening now. It means focusing your full attention and awareness on the information you receive through your senses at that moment.

Areas of My Life	Actions I Do Out of Habit	How I Can Be More Mindful
Family		
Health		
Friends		
Work		
Leisure time		
Religion		
Material possessions		
Politics		
Other		

Fully Present Quotations

Put check marks by the quotes that you feel would inspire you to stay in the present. You can cut the quote out and post by your computer or on your refrigerator or tuck it in your wallet. At the bottom of the page, write why those particular quotes speak to you.

- *You don't need endless time and perfect conditions. Do it now. Do it for twenty minutes and watch your heart start beating.* ~ **Barbara Sher**

- *You can clutch the past so tightly to your chest that it leaves your arms too full to embrace the present.* ~ **Jan Glidewell**

- *If you are still talking about what you did yesterday, you haven't done much today.* ~ **Author Unknown**

- *Don't let yesterday use up too much of today.* ~ **Cherokee Indian Proverb**

- *It is only possible to live happily-ever-after on a day-to-day basis.* ~ **Margaret Bonnano**

- *Yesterday is history. Tomorrow is a mystery. And today? Today is a gift. That's why we call it the present.* ~ **Babatunde Olatunji**

- *I have realized that the past and future are real illusions, that they exist in the present, which is what there is and all there is.* ~ **Alan Watts**

- *We are always getting ready to live but never living.* ~ **Ralph Waldo Emerson**

- *Children have neither past nor future; they enjoy the present, which very few of us do.* ~ **Jean de la Bruyere**

- *The past, the present and the future are really one – they are today.* ~ **Harriet Beecher Stowe**

- *The best thing about the future is that it comes only one day at a time.* ~ **Abraham Lincoln**

I selected the quotation(s) above because

_____

_____

_____

_____

_____

Meaning and Purpose

People are constantly seeking ways to find meaning and purpose in their lives. A sense of purpose is necessary for physical health and emotional well-being. Work provides us with a certain sense of purpose, but often has to be supplemented with meaningful leisure activities. In the following table, list some of the work and leisure activities that bring you meaning and a sense of purpose.

I find meaning in these activities at work . . .
Ex. Working with my team of co-workers on an important project.

I find meaning in these leisure activities . . .
Ex. Creating a sand castle on a sunny day at the beach with my children.

Meaning and Life Purpose Quotations

Finding your meaning and life purpose and your deepest life intentions can help you to move with greater focus and clarity every day of your life. Check one or two quotes to which you can relate and at the bottom of the page, write your reaction and thoughts about the quote(s) you selected.

- *The question is not whether we will die, but how we will live.* ~ **Borysenko, Joan**

- *The purpose of life is to live a life of purpose.* ~ **Richard Leider**

- *Develop an interest in life as you see it; the people, things, literature, music-the world is so rich, simply throbbing with rich treasures, beautiful souls and interesting people. Forget yourself.* ~ **Henry Miller**

- *Seeing yourself as you want to be is the key to personal growth.* ~ **Anonymous**

- *Purpose serves as a principle around which to organize our lives.* ~ **Anonymous**

- *Life is a promise; fulfill it.* ~ **Mother Theresa**

- *Great minds have purposes, little minds have wishes.* ~ **Washington Irving**

- *First say to yourself what you would be; and then do what you have to do.* ~ **Epictetus**

- *One needs something to believe in, something for which one can have whole-hearted enthusiasm. One needs to feel that one's life has meaning, that one is needed in this world.* ~ **Hannah Senesh**

- *Many people have a wrong idea of what constitutes true happiness. It is not attained through self-gratification, but through fidelity to a worthy purpose.* ~ **Helen Keller**

- *I'm doing what I think I was put on this earth to do. And I'm really grateful to have something that I'm passionate about and that I think is profoundly important.*
  ~ **Marian Wright Edelman**

My reactions and thoughts about the quotes checked . . .

_____

_____

_____

_____

_____

_____

_____

_____

_____

Ways You Can be More Mindful*

- Eat slowly and mindfully and enjoy the taste of the food.

- Be mindful as you listen to music – listen and enjoy it as fully as you can in all of its nuances, levels and sound variations.

- Become a good listener and listen intently to others. Truly listening as someone speaks is a gift.

- Take a moment or two every day to look around and find beauty. Seek an object or event of beauty that you have never noticed before.

- Develop a heightened awareness of your body – identify those areas where you experience physical reactions to tensions and stresses in your life.

- Engage in mindful meditation by concentrating on your breaths to calm your scattered mind.

- Observe your mind clearly as you speak and watch for your intentions to help or harm others through your words or body language.

*Adapted from Walsh, R. (1999). Essential Spirituality. New York: John Wiley & Sons.

Meaning and Purpose . . .

- allow us to discover absorbing activities in our lives.

- assist us to find the balance between selflessness and selfishness.

- help us become more in touch with ourselves and more absorbed in life.

- help us become selfless because we are so absorbed in a purpose.

- help us to identify, explore and utilize our potentials.

- provide us with a roadmap for the future.

- provide us with life satisfaction.

- support health and survival.

SECTION VI

The Last Chapter

of

*Discovering Your Spiritual Path
Workbook*

Is the Next Chapter

of

YOUR
Spiritual Path

Self Awareness & Personal Spiritual Growth

Personal growth is an integral part of our purpose of life. With self-awareness we take charge. We wake up to our amazing potential. We uncover our creativity, talent and wisdom that is already inside of us.

After completing the activities in this book, what are three things you have learned about yourself?

1) _____

_____

2) _____

_____

3) _____

_____

Are there obstacles you have found along your spiritual path? What or who are they?

_____

_____

_____

_____

_____

What have you learned about spirituality?

_____

_____

_____

_____

_____

What will be your next step?

_____

_____

_____

_____

_____

A lotus blossom
symbolizes enlightenment.

With crayons, markers or color pencil, color and/or write in, around or through the petals of this lotus blossom - the various ways you feel you have experienced enlightenment, or learned something new - that will help toward your spiritual well-being.

In the space below, doodle, draw or write anything
that comes to your mind about spirituality.

Your Linked Chain of Spirituality Resources

After completing the *Discovering Your Spiritual Path Workbook*, you now are aware that you have an abundance of spiritual resources available to you along your Spiritual Journey.

On each chain link, write a resource that opens a possibility for you (flowers in the back yard, a special person, sacred writings, etc). If you would prefer, cut out your own paper strips and link them with glue. Then write each resource on a link. As you continue on your path, continue to add more resources that link you to a wealth of opportunities.

My Personal Spirituality Definition

_____
(my name)

Our view or definition of success, happiness and peace may change over time. So may our definition of spirituality. Based on everything you have learned about yourself in this workbook, it is time for you to compose your present definition of spirituality. Because spirituality is such a unique concept, your definition will be unique to you. As you grow and change, so might your definition of spirituality. From time to time, take a moment to reflect on your definition of spirituality and rewrite it to reflect your newest definition.

Save this page and use the space below to notice how your definition of spirituality changes over time.

My Spirituality Definition Today   Date _____

_____
_____
_____
_____

Three Months from Now ~ My Spirituality Definition Date _____

_____
_____
_____
_____

One Year from Now ~ My Spirituality Definition   Date _____

_____
_____
_____
_____

Spirituality Books

These books were recommended by many of the participants of our spirituality survey. Similar to the other components of spirituality, seeking out varied spiritual messages is well worth the search.*

Albom, M. *Tuesdays with Morrie: An Old Man, a Young Man, and Life's Greatest Lesson.* Bantam Books

Bach, R. and R. Munson *Jonathan Livingston Seagull.* Simon and Schuster Benson, P. Vision Awakening Your Potential to Create a Better World. Templeton Press

Breathnach, S. *Simple Abundance: A Daybook of Comfort and Joy.* Grand Central Publications

Bucke, M. D. *Cosmic Consciousness: A Study in the Evolution of the Human Mind.* Cosimo Classics

Capacchione, L. *Lighten Up Your Body ~ Lighten Up Your Life.* Newcastle Publishing

Chodron, P. *Places that Scare You, Start Where You Are, When Things Fall Apart* and *Wisdom of No Escape.* Shambhala Publications

Chopra, D. *Life After Death: The Burden of Proof.* Random House

Chopra, D. *Seven Spiritual Laws of Success: A Practical Guide to the Fulfillment of Your Dreams.* ReadHowYouWant

Choquette, S. *Soul Lessons and Soul Purpose: A Channeled Guide to Why You Are Here.* Hay House

Coerr, E. *Sadako and the Thousand Paper Cranes.* Penguin Group Coles, R. The Spiritual Life of Children. Houghton Mifflin

Cornfield, J. and M. Hansen *Chicken Soup for the Soul.* HCI Chicken Soup

Cotner, J. *Serenity Prayers — Prayers, Poems, and Prose to Soothe Your Soul.* Andrews McMeel

Dreher, D. *The Tao of Inner Peace.* Penguin House

Dunn, D. and W. Crumpler *Cusco: the Gateway to Inner Wisdom.* Planeta Publ. Corp.

Dyer, W. *Change Your Thoughts — Change Your Life: Living the Wisdom of the Tao.* Hay House

Epstein, M. *Thoughts Without A Thinker.* Basic Books

Fitzpatrick, J.G. *Small Wonder: How to Answer your Child's Impossible Questions about Life.* Penguin.

Fitzpatrick, J.G. *Something More: Nurturing your Child's Spiritual Growth.* Penguin

Fox, M. *Original Blessing.* Penguin Group

Fuchs-Kreimer, N. *Deepening Ordinary and Extraordinary Events into Sacred Occasions.* Jewish Lights Publishing

Gafni, M. *Soul Prints: Your Path to Fulfillment.* Simon and Schuster

Garland, D. *Sacred Stories of Ordinary Families.* Jossey Bass

Gibran, K. *The Prophet.* Knopf Doubleday Publishing

Gilbert, E. *Eat, Pray, Love: One Woman's Search for Everything Across Italy, India and Indonesia.* Penguin Books

Gray, E. *Sacred Dimensions of Women's Experience.* Roundtable Press

Hagen, S. *Buddhism Plain and Simple.* Bantam Books

Hall, M. *The Secret Teachings of All Ages.* Wilder Publications

Hanh, T. N. *Peace Is Every Step: The Path of Mindfulness in Everyday Life.* Bantam Books

Hawkins, D. *Power vs. Force: The Hidden Determinants of Human Behavior.* Hay House

Hirschfield, B. *You Don't Have to Be Wrong for Me to Be Right: Finding Faith Without Fanaticism.* Crown Publishing Group

Hoff, B. *The Pao of Pooh.* Penguin Group

Hopkins, E., R. Kelley, K. Bentley, and J. Murphy *Working With Groups on Spiritual Themes.* Whole Person Associates

Ingerman, S. *Soul Retrieval: Mending the Fragmented Self.* HarperCollins

Jenkins, E. *The Initiation: A Woman's Spiritual Adventure in the Heart of the Andes.* Berkeley Books

Joseph, S. *Loving Every Child: Wisdom for Parents; the Words of Janusz Korczak.* Algonquin Books

Kabat-Zinn, J. *Wherever You Go, There You Are: Mindfulness Meditation on Everyday Life.* Hyperion

Katie, B. and S. Mitchell *A Thousand Names for Joy: Living in Harmony with the Way Things Are.* Three Rivers Press

Kirkpatrick, S. *Edgar Cayce: An American Prophet.* Penguin Group

Kornfield, J. *A Path with Heart: A Guide Through the Perils and Promises of Spiritual Life.* Bantam Books

Kula, I, Loewenthal, L. *Yearnings: Embracing the Sacred Messiness of Life.* Hyperion

LaGrand, L. *Love Lives On: Learning from the Extraordinary Encounters of the Bereaved.* Penguin Group

Lama, HH The D and H. Cutler *Art of Happiness: A Handbook for Living.* Penguin Group

Lama, HH The D. *Universe in a Single Atom: The Convergence of Science and Spirituality.* Broadway Books

Lama, HH The D, V. Chan *Wisdom of Forgiveness.* Penguin Group

Larkin, G. *Stumbling Toward Enlightenment.* Ten Speed Press

Lash, J. *The Seekers Handbook: The Complete Guide to Spritual Pathfinding.* Harmony Books

Lerner, M. *Spirit Matters.* Hampton Roads Publishing

Levine, S. *Guided Meditations, Explorations and Healings.* Knopf Doubleday Publishing Group

Lewis, R. *Living by wonder: The Imaginative Life of Childhood.* Parabola Books

Lionni, L. *Frederick.* Random House Children's Books

Lipton, B. *Biology of Belief: Unleashing the Power of Consciousness, Matter, & Miracles.* Hay House

Matthiessen, P., P. Iyer *Snow Leopard.* Penguin Group

Mykoff, M. *Empty Chair: Timeless Wisdom from a Hassidic Master Rebbe Nachman of Breslov.* Jewish Lights Publishing

Myss, C. *Sacred Contracts: Awakening Your Divine Potential.* Random House

Newton, M. *Journey of Souls: New Case Studies of Life Between Lives.* Llewellyn Worldwide

Oriah *The Invitation.* HarperSanFrancisco

Oxenhandler, N. *Wishing Year: A House, A Man, My Soul: A Memoir of Fulfilled Desire.* Random House

Prather, H. *The Little Book of Letting Go: A Revolutionary 30-Day Program.* Red Wheel/Weiser

Radmacher, M. *Lean Forward into Your Life: Begin Each Day as If it Were on Purpose.* Conari Press

Remen, R. *My Grandfather's Blessings: Stories of Strength, Refuge and Belonging.* Penguin Group

Rodegast, P. *Emmanuel's Book: A Manual for Living Comfortably in the Cosmos.* Bantam Books

Salzberg, S. Faith: *Trusting Your Own Deepest Experience.* Penguin Group

Sanford, A. *The Healing Gifts of the Spirit.* HarperCollins

Schachter-Shalomi, Z., R. Miller *From Age-ing to Sage-ing: A Profound New Vision of Growing Older.* Warner Books

Schlitz, M., M. Vieten and Tina Amorok *Living Deeply: The Art and Science of Transformation in Everyday Life.* New Harbinger

Schuette, K. *Soul-Purpose: Awaken Your Perfect Self.* Author House

Shapiro, R. *Sacred Art of Lovingkindness: Preparing to Practice.* Jewish Lights Publishing

Siegel, B. Love, *Medicine & Miracles.* HarperCollins Publishers

Singer, M. *Untethered Soul: The Journey Beyond Yourself.* New Harbinger Publishing

Stonehouse, C. *Joining Children on the Spiritual Journey.* Baker Book House

Suzuki, S. *Zen Mind, Beginner's Mind: Informal Talks on Zen Meditation and Practice.* Shambhala Publications

Thurston, M., C. Fazel *Edgar Cayce Handbook for Creating Your Future.* Random House

Tolle, E. *A New Earth, Awakening To Your Life's Purpose.* Penguin Group

Vaughn, F. and R. Walsh *Gifts from a Course in Miracles.* Penguin Group

Wakefield, D. *Story of Your Life: Writing A Spiritual Autobiography.* Beacon Press

Weiss, A. *Beginning Mindfulness — Learning the Way of Awareness.* New World Library Penguin Group

Weiss, B. *Messages from the Masters: Tapping into the Power of Love.* Grand Central Publishing

Wood, D. *Old Turtle.* Scholastic Inc.

Yust, K.M. *Real Kids, Real Faith: Practices for Nurturing Children's Spiritual Lives.* Jossey-Bass

Yust, K.M., M. Johnson, N. Aostre, S. E. Sasso, E. Roehlkepartain *Nurturing child and adolescent spirituality: Perspectives from the World's Religious Traditions.* Rowman & Littlefield

Zukav, G. *The Heart of the Soul: Emotional Awareness.* Simon and Schuster

Zukav, G. *The Seat of the Soul.* Simon and Schuster

*Several of these authors have other spirituality titles available that are not listed. There are many other authors and books about spirituality that are not represented on this list.

WholePerson

Whole Person Associates is the leading publisher of training resources for professionals who empower people to create and maintain healthy lifestyles. Our creative resources will help you work effectively with your clients in the areas of stress management, wellness promotion, mental health and life skills.

Please visit us at our web site: **WholePerson.com**. You can check out our entire line of products, place an order, request our print catalog, and sign up for our monthly special notifications.

Whole Person Associates

800-247-6789